LEWIS CARROLL

PHOTOGRAPHER

by
Helmut Gernsheim

Revised Edition

DOVER PUBLICATIONS, INC.

NEW YORK

Published in Canada by General Publishing Company, Ltd., 30 Lesmill Road, Don Mills, Toronto, Ontario.
Published in the United Kingdom by Constable and Company, Ltd., 10 Orange Street, London WC 2.

This Dover edition, first published in 1969, is an unabridged and revised republication of the work originally published by Max Parrish & Co., Limited, London, in 1949. A new preface has been written by the author for this edition.

Standard Book Number: 486-22327-2
Library of Congress Catalog Card Number: 68-8045

Manufactured in the United States of America
Dover Publications, Inc.
180 Varick Street
New York, N. Y. 10014

In honour
and loving memory of

ALISON EAMES GERNSHEIM

through twenty-seven years
of marriage   a wonderful companion,
ideal   collaborator and
wise   counsellor

Preface to the Dover Edition

APART FROM this new Preface and the incorporation of the Addenda to the Second Edition, published in 1950, in the main body of the book, only a few minor alterations became necessary due to change of ownership of certain albums and photographs.

The publication of my book drew attention to the existence of the unpublished diaries of Lewis Carroll, with the result that Miss F.M. Dodgson and her sisters were besieged by biographers for all kinds of information. As the copying out of extracts for me had proved a slow and tedious task, they decided on the simplest course—the publication of the complete diaries, in 1953. Despite the very able editing of Roger Lancelyn Green, the general expectation that these two volumes would provide a new mine of information was not fulfilled. In particular, no new light has been thrown upon Lewis Carroll's friendship with, or rather love for, Alice Liddell. It now appears that the diaries from May 1858 to May 1862 were not lost in the move of Lewis Carroll's nieces from London to Leamington Spa, but had been destroyed by his over-conscientious nephew-biographer Stuart Dodgson Collingwood. Nevertheless, I learned soon after the publication of my book from Alice's son, Wing Commander Caryl Hargreaves, that Lewis Carroll had wanted to marry his mother but had been rejected by her parents. The rebuff received from Dean and Mrs. Liddell, who considered the middle-aged and somewhat eccentric mathematics lecturer of modest means a far from desirable suitor, was the disappointment alluded to by Collingwood. Thus the veil has been lifted at last from one of the most important incidents in Lewis Carroll's life, which had given rise to much speculation.

Through my book, I had the pleasure of meeting several of Lewis Carroll's child friends—including the nonagenarian Mrs. Bickersteth, the subject of Plate 59—who vividly remembered the delight of being dressed up or the boredom of being posed in the nude. They were also able to throw light on Lewis Carroll's decision to give up photography in 1880 (see pages 80–81). It seems that despite his precaution of photographing girls in the nude only in the presence of the mother or another adult woman, a scandal did develop in Oxford in 1880, which decided Lewis Carroll to abandon his hobby altogether. This bears out my feeling that the reason for his decision lay outside the field of photo-technique.

Lastly, reference must be made to the two photographs which I have substituted in this edition for the original Plate 45 (Farringford) and Plate 64 (Ethel Hatch). Both the new pictures are much stronger and more characteristic of Lewis Carroll's best work. The photograph of Alice Liddell [Plate 45] was presented to me by the late Wing Commander Caryl Hargreaves. It was taken by Lewis Carroll in the garden of the Deanery about 1859–60. The charming composition "St. George and the Dragon" [Plate 64] was staged by Lewis Carroll about 1874 in his rooms at Christ Church, the models being Xie Kitchin and her brothers. The original negative of this and some other photographs of Xie Kitchin were presented to me by her son, and are now in the Gernsheim Collection at the University of Texas, Austin, Texas.

I am very grateful to Professor John W. Meaney, Curator of the Gernsheim Collection, for making available the prints for the present edition.

Helmut Gernsheim

Castagnola—Lugano
1969

Preface to the First Edition

IT IS a remarkable coincidence that while collecting material for my biography of Julia Margaret Cameron my attention was drawn to an album of another great mid-Victorian amateur photographer—Lewis Carroll. Turning its pages, I was struck first by the fertility of his imagination; later I became aware that each picture possessed a strong individual character, and the more I studied the 115 photographs it contains, the more I was convinced that here was a genius at work, the like of which is rare in nineteenth-century photography.

Between myself and possession of the album stood only its price, and once that difficulty was overcome, curiosity led to eager research, for quite frankly until then Lewis Carroll, photographer, had been a stranger to me.

I consulted the leading histories of photography and studied the photographic literature of the last century for information; I sought it with thimbles, I sought it with care, I pursued it with forks and hope, but Dodgson's name and his pseudonym remained as elusive as the Snark.

The voluminous literature which has appeared about Lewis Carroll in the half-century since his death added little to my knowledge of this subject. It is true that nearly every one of his many biographers made a passing reference to his photography, and one or two even proffered the information that it was his chief hobby, but when they ventured beyond that simple statement of fact into the world of surmise they often fell into layman's errors.

There the matter rested, until several months later Lewis Carroll cut once more across my researches on Mrs. Cameron's photography. An article in the *Century Magazine* mentioned his work alongside that of other prominent Victorian amateur photographers, the writer quoting a few entries from one of Lewis Carroll's diaries to substantiate his remarks. Here, then, at last was the golden key which was to open up the source of information—but it took me, like Alice, some time to find the right door.

The nieces of Lewis Carroll kindly consented to extract from their uncle's unpublished diaries all entries relating to photography, with permission to publish anything I thought of sufficient interest, and I have augmented my selection with notes and explanations to sketch in the necessary background. Lewis Carroll kept a diary from 1854 to the end of 1897, but the entries concerning photography extend only from 1856 to 1880. To enable the reader to arrive at a proper evaluation of his achievements as a pioneer of amateur photography, I have prefaced the extracts with an account of the state of photography in England prior to and concurrent with Lewis Carroll's own work.

A consideration of Lewis Carroll's friendships with children is equally indispensable for an understanding of his photography, which is so closely bound up with this most important aspect of his life that to ignore the human side would inevitably result in an incomplete picture.

Occasionally I have also drawn upon Lewis Carroll's voluminous correspondence—he wrote about two thousand letters a year, and with his characteristic fussiness in pigeon-holing every detail of his life, kept a letter register for thirty-seven years, which gives a précis of every letter sent and received, and at the time of his death contained 98,721 cross-references.

Since it is impossible to discuss Lewis Carroll, photographer, without referring to his writing on photography, a reprint has been included of all his literary works which have any bearing on the subject: *Photography Extraordinary*, *Hiawatha's Photographing*, *A Photographer's Day Out* and *The Ladye's History* from *The Legend of "Scotland"*.

Lastly, the reader will find a catalogue of Lewis Carroll's photograph albums, as far as they could be traced, and a complete list of the distinguished men and women who sat to him.

Our understanding of Lewis Carroll is as yet by no means complete. Countless writers have given us reminiscences or have dealt with his life and literary work. We have been provided with a fascinating selection of Lewis Carroll's letters to his child friends; and a valuable psycho-analytical study of Carroll/Dodgson, the paradox, in a recent biography. However, so far no one has been tempted to give us an appreciation of Lewis Carroll's graphic art, which far surpasses most of the work which other illustrators contributed to his books. Above all, it is to be hoped that the future will see the unexpurgated publication of Lewis Carroll's diaries, for it is natural to assume that they might throw new light on a number of matters about which we are still in the dark: I have in mind particularly the event to which his conscientious nephew-biographer Stuart Dodgson Collingwood merely referred as "the shadow of some disappointment which lay over Lewis Carroll's life", adding with true Victorian chivalry, "Those who loved him would not wish to lift the veil from these dead sanctities, nor would any purpose be served by so doing." Perhaps it would, after all.

May 1949   Helmut Gernsheim

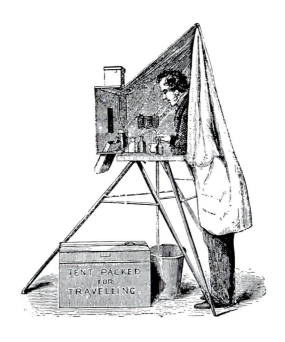

TENT PACKED FOR TRAVELLING

Contents

1

Photography—The New Art

On 19th August 1839 details of Daguerre's photographic process were revealed to an excited audience at the Académie des Sciences, Paris. With a grand gesture the French Government gave the invention free to the whole world, and no one suspected that five days earlier Daguerre

1

had managed, through an agent, to patent his process in England and Wales.

Henry Fox Talbot's discovery of photogenic drawing, made known six months previously, though free from patent restrictions, was very limited in scope, having little useful application except to botany and microscopy. His first *practical* process, the calotype, Talbot protected by a patent in February 1841.

The nature of the daguerreotype was such that it found no favour with amateurs; at any rate, not a single instance of a British amateur daguerreotypist has come to my notice. The cost of the materials, the complicated manipulation, the small size of the picture, the impossibility of multiplying it, the delicacy of the silvered surface—necessitating its being carefully mounted in a case—were all deterrent factors.

In London the daguerreotype process was practised only by a few professionals of means and ability, who had paid the patentee very high fees for the right to practise the process. A few more bought the sole right for certain provincial towns, or even for whole counties, and carefully guarded their monopoly.

The calotype process had only two or three adherents amongst professionals, since the public, used to miniatures, preferred the minute detail of the daguerreotype to the broader effects of the calotype.

The number of amateurs who took out a licence from Fox Talbot is also astonishingly small, considering that the process was simple and the materials cheap, and it was capable of producing large paper negatives from which an almost unlimited number of copies could be printed. The explanation for this state of affairs lies in the conditions laid down in the licences. The would-be amateur was informed that he was forbidden to give away any prints to friends without first obtaining Fox Talbot's leave, that to sell any would lead to an injunction, and that if he should for any reason incur the displeasure of the patentee, the licence might be withdrawn at a moment's notice. Maybe there was no risk of incurring the patentee's displeasure if his instructions were conscientiously followed: the fact remains that few people cared to take up photography under such conditions.

Such was the state of photography throughout the eighteen-forties, but in 1851 occurred two events which contributed greatly to the rise of amateur photography. It is a curious fact that they followed each

2

other very closely, although there was no connection between them.

In March 1851 the collodion or wet-plate process was made known to the world by Frederick Scott Archer, and since—apart from constituting a great improvement on previous methods—it was the first photographic process free from patent restrictions, the hope arose that it would fulfil the amateur's dream of taking pictures of whatever he wished, and doing as he pleased with them.

The second factor was the Great Exhibition of 1851, which was not only the first international exhibition, but also included the first important photographic exhibition. As a result, lovers and students of the art in all parts of England were brought into contact with the work of other photographers. Ideas and practical methods were exchanged, and since the pleasure of giving and receiving instruction was mutual, it was proposed to unite "all those gentlemen whose tastes have led them to the cultivation of this branch of natural science" in a society with a fixed meeting-place and a proper organisation similar to that of other learned societies.

However, all efforts in this direction were thwarted for the time being because no agreement could be reached with Fox Talbot on the question of patent rights. Eventually, in July 1852, he was persuaded, through the united efforts of the Presidents of the Royal Society and of the Royal Academy, to relinquish his patent rights—except in the case of portraits for sale.

This exception did not seem a serious obstacle at first, because the collodion process, which superseded Fox Talbot's own, as well as the daguerreotype, appeared to offer a good alternative. The remark of the *Illustrated London News*,[1] "To Mr. Archer the public owe a debt of gratitude as at last giving them one process for portraits which can be practised without fear of the law", met with agreement from everybody —except the patentee of the calotype process. *He* claimed that the newly discovered collodion process was only a variation or modification of the calotype, and proceeded with injunctions to restrain those who were exhibiting and selling portraits taken by the collodion process without having first obtained a licence from him. Photographers lay low for a time until, in December 1854, a courageous professional,

[1] 28th August 1852.

Silvester Laroche, successfully resisted Talbot's claim in a lawsuit. Subsequently Talbot abandoned his petition for renewal of his calotype patent for a further fourteen years, and so by February 1855 photography in England was at last free from the shackles in which he and Daguerre had placed it. (The daguerreotype patent had already run its term by 1853.)

From then on, the progress of photography was incredibly rapid. The perfection of the collodion process made it a really popular pursuit, and with mistaken ideas as to the ease of the new method, large numbers of amateurs purchased the necessary apparatus, and some became "professionals" overnight, without having the faintest idea of the principles of the art. Never was a taste so catholic as that which united in a new fraternity "the pilgrims of the sun". Men of all tastes, ranks and professions seemed seized with the mania. Even Queen Victoria and Prince Albert had a photographic darkroom constructed at Windsor Castle, and became well skilled in the "black art"—fit patrons for the Photographic Society, founded shortly before.

The remarkable popularity of photography can best be measured by the number of pictures hung at the Society's exhibitions. Nearly 1,500 photographs were shown at the first exhibition in December 1853; the following year, 721; in January 1856, 606; in December 1856, 712, and this figure remained more or less constant throughout the fifties and sixties.

Portraiture was still almost exclusively in the hands of professionals, while amateurs delighted in landscapes, town views and architecture. There was not always a clearly defined division between amateurs and professionals: many so-called amateurs published and sold their views through dealers, while quite a proportion of professionals continued to carry on their original occupation as well, often returning to it altogether after some years.

The prominent part played by photography in contemporary life can best be gauged from the lengthy discussions and detailed exhibition reviews by art critics, which appeared in all the national papers and magazines. Completely carried away by the new art, one critic expressed his enthusiasm with a pomposity which must be read to be believed.

Photography is an enormous stride forward in the region of art. The old

4

world was well nigh exhausted with its wearisome mothers and children called Madonnas; its everlasting dead bodies called Entombments; its wearisome nudities called Nymphs and Venuses; its endless porters called Marses and Vulcans; its dead Christianity and its deader Paganism. Here was a world with the soil fainting and exhausted; worn by man into barrenness, overcrowded, over-housed, over-taxed, over-known. Then all at once breaks a small light in the far West, and a new world slowly widens to our sight—new sky, new earth, new flowers, a very heaven compared with the old earth. Here is room for man and beast for centuries to come, fresh pastures, virgin earth, untouched forests; here is land never trodden but by the angels on the day of Creation. This new land is Photography, Art's youngest and fairest child; no rival of the old family, no struggler for worn-out birthrights, but heir to a new heaven and a new earth, found by itself, and to be left to its own children.

For photography there are new secrets to conquer, new difficulties to overcome, new Madonnas to invent, new ideals to imagine. There will be perhaps photograph Raphaels, photograph Titians, founders of new empires, and not subverters of the old.[1]

PHOTOGRAPHY FOR THE MILLION

Unfortunately there are no statistics for the growth of amateur photography, but the census of professional photographers provides a fair indication. In 1841 photography was not recorded as an occupation at all, but we know that there were at least three professional establishments in London alone. No doubt at that time their proprietors were still entered under their former occupations. In 1851 the census for Great Britain included 51 professional photographers. Ten years later the number had increased to 2,534, which is certainly an understatement, since it does not take account of the legion of petty dabblers, or the thousands of employees engaged in the trade. In London in the mid-fifties there were more than 150 photographic "glass houses", thirty-five of them crowded into Regent Street.[2] "Scarcely a favourable spot for the practice of the art is left untenanted," runs the report of the Jury on Photography at the International Exhibition in 1862. Every town of note, and even some remote villages, now boasted one or

---

[1] From the review of the Photographic Exhibition 1856/1857, *Photographic Journal*, 21st February 1857, p. 217.

[2] The name Glasshouse Street still serves as a reminder of the heyday of photography.

more photographers, and travelling photographic vans made the round of outlying country districts.

The consumption of photographic materials was quite fabulous. To mention only one item—amusing because of its topical interest for our diet—one London firm used upwards of half a million eggs annually to obtain albumen which was employed in the preparation of positive photographic printing paper!

In 1857 the *carte-de-visite* portrait was introduced into England by a French firm of photographic dealers. This kind of portrait had been invented and patented by the Parisian photographer Disdéri in 1854. The new fashion of having a small portrait on a mount the size of a visiting-card did not at first find favour in fashionable circles, but established itself quickly with low-class photographers, since the poorer clientele, who could not afford to pay a guinea for one large portrait, were well pleased to have half a dozen cards for a few shillings.

No longer was photography the art for the privileged: it had become the art for the million. "Photographic portraiture is the best feature of the fine arts for the million that the ingenuity of man has yet devised. It has in this sense swept away many of the illiberal distinctions of rank and wealth, so that the poor man who possesses but a few shillings can command as perfect a lifelike portrait of his wife or child as Sir Thomas Lawrence painted for the most distinguished sovereigns of Europe."[1]

Whereas in the eighteen-forties many miniature painters and other artists had turned to photography for their livelihood, we now find the unhappy union, particularly in suburbia and seaside resorts, of photography with ice-cream and roast-chestnut shops, with barbers and tobacconists, with Greenwich and Gravesend tea-and-shrimp rooms. Naturally this brought with it a general lowering of standards since the profit-making angle attracted to photography many cheap traders who had no other motive but to exploit the boom.

Under the title "Art Progress" *Punch*[2] published a delightful cartoon showing two rival photographic portrait shops side by side, and four photographers touting for sitters, seizing a passing lady: "Now, Mum! Take off yer 'ead for sixpence, or yer 'ole body for a shillin'!" *Punch*

---

[1] *Photographic News*, 18th October 1861, p. 500.

[2] 2nd May 1857.

did not exaggerate. "Invitations to have one's portrait taken at sixpence, with a discount of 18 per cent on taking a dozen, are numerous."[1]

In May 1859 Napoleon III's visit to Disdéri's studio made the *carte* portrait fashionable in France. Popularisation in England began in May the following year, when one of the front-rank portrait photographers, American-born J. E. Mayall, was honoured with a command to visit Buckingham Palace and take *carte* portraits of the Queen, Prince Albert and other members of the Royal family. Hundreds of thousands of these pictures were sold in no time, for everyone wanted to possess a lifelike representation of the universally loved Queen and her family. Their unparalleled success gave great impetus to this branch of photography, through the understandable desire of every photographer to reap an equally rich harvest with other distinguished personalities. They in their turn were only too eager to follow the example set by the Royal family, and to see their portraits exhibited in shop windows alongside those of their sovereign.

Public figures were constantly pestered for a sitting. In the trade they were termed "sure cards"; for each time a famous man consented to sit, several hundred pounds went into the pocket of the lucky photographer. Since tens of thousands of copies had to be on the market quickly in order to satisfy the great demand, and to crush all possible competition, a number of negatives were required to print from. It is reported that the London Stereoscopic Company took no fewer than four dozen negatives of Lord Palmerston at one sitting.[2]

Though no one had the bad taste to leave his portrait as a visiting-card, which was Disdéri's original idea, by the end of 1860 it had become fashionable to have one's *carte* portrait taken and to exchange it with friends. Thus for once we find the remarkable phenomenon that a fashion established itself in society long after it had been popular with every Tom, Dick and Harry.

Never was there a period in the history of photography when such large incomes were earned by able and enterprising professional photographers. We are told that Disdéri took no less than £48,000 a

---

[1] *Photographic News*, 24th September 1858, p. 32.

[2] *Ibid.*, 5th August 1864, p. 383.

year in the early sixties. Here in England nothing like such spectacular receipts were realised. Mayall led English professionals with £12,000 a year. Marion & Co., the largest photographic dealers, stated that they paid him no less than £35,000 for his photographs of the Royal family in the course of a few years.

The most successful provincial photographer was Canadian-born Oliver Sarony, who settled in Scarborough in 1857. He reckoned to make about £10,000 a year, following closely on Mayall's heels. His establishment was in the most fashionable part of the town. A broad flight of steps led up to the imposing entrance of his 120-foot-long "palace", furnished in Louis Quinze style—"the embodiment of good taste and costly elegance". People flocked from all over the country to be photographed by Sarony. His business brought a lot of money to the town, and in gratitude the town council named the square in which his establishment stood "Sarony Square".

Even a French aristocrat, Camille Silvy, stooped for a few years to the lucrative business of portrait photography. He bought a studio in Porchester Terrace, London, in 1859, and within eighteen months employed forty men in his business. Gifted with exquisite taste and the Frenchman's instinctive understanding of the fair sex, he ran a series, "The Beauties of England", which for some years swamped the market. Silvy soon made a fortune, and when the *carte* mania began to fall off he retired to his ancestral château.

Several million *cartes* were taken annually in England; so great, indeed, was the number that more than one Chancellor of the Exchequer is said to have considered following America's example and materially adding to the national income by means of a small tax on these productions.

No Victorian drawing-room was complete without its photograph album. Political and religious associations, party and piety, found ample scope in the morocco-bound volume. The first few pages were usually devoted to the Royal family, which in the Victorian album did duty as grace before meat. Then followed the public men one admired, and lastly the family circle and friends. So the album at the same time served as an illustrated book of genealogy and expressed a form of hero-worship. It was an excellent means of whiling away the awkward half-hour before dinner, indicating to visitors the tastes and prejudices

8

of their host. The portrait of Bishop Wilberforce or of T. H. Huxley, of Charles Kingsley or of Father Newman, of Disraeli or of John Bright, might act as a beacon to the cautious sailor in the narrow seas of small talk; while in the way of suggestions and hints for that same dreary time of emptiness of mind and stomach alike, there was nothing better than to fall back on the pictorial household gods on the table, which were sure to offer some opportunity of showing off one's knowledge of things in general and of the contemporary scene in particular.

Soon tastes became more catholic, prompted by the caprice of fashion, and by the curiosity inherent in human nature about the appearance of celebrities of all kinds. Turning the leaves of the album, the visitor would find premiers and prima donnas, preachers and pugilists, ambassadors and actors, all rubbing shoulders in perfect *égalité* and *fraternité*.

When in time the ordinary photograph album began to pall, the musical album provided a welcome touch of novelty. What could be more charming than to have a musical box concealed in the album which started to play its tinkling tunes when the book was opened!

To me, I frankly admit, an old photograph album is something fascinating. It is so amusing to see the complacent expressions of the sitters and their affected poses; to study the vagaries of fashion and the photographic trickery it all entailed.

PORTRAIT PHOTOGRAPHY – A NEW INDUSTRY

Photographers were swamped with orders and were tempted to give too many sittings. A contemporary photographic journal recorded as a praiseworthy feat that one operator had taken ninety-seven negatives in eight hours—just under five minutes apiece.

Under these conditions of mass production, is it to be wondered at that the poses are stereotyped? Few photographers had more than two or three "sets" for posing; so, on the occasion cited above, something like thirty-two people must have been subjected to precisely the same treatment: that is to say, they were placed in the same position, in the same light, against the same pillar or balustrade—and in all probability they have the same expression.

His head screwed into a vice, the sitter was told to look at an indicated spot on the wall, and to keep still. Thus posed, he would regard the further operations with much the same feelings of distrust as he would those of a dentist. His breathing would become heavier and quicker as the critical moment of uncapping the lens drew near, his heart would beat visibly beneath his waistcoat, and a hazy film seemed to form before his eyes. Just when he felt least like it, he was asked to put on a pleasant smile.

> Apollo's agent on earth, when your attitude's right,
> Your collar adjusted, your locks in their place,
> Just seizes one moment of favouring light
> And utters three sentences—"Now it's begun"—
> "It's going on now, sir"—and "Now it is done".
> And lo! as I live, there's the cut of your face
> On a silvery plate
> Unerring as fate,
> Worked off in celestial and strange mezzotint,
> A little resembling an elderly print.
> "Well, I *never!*" all cry; "it is cruelly like you!"
> But Truth is unpleasant
> To prince and to peasant.
> You recollect Lawrence and think of the graces
> That Chalon and company give to their faces,
> The face you have worn fifty years doesn't strike you![1]

There was no attempt at characterisation, no endeavour to record what Julia Margaret Cameron called "the greatness of the inner, as well as the features of the outer man". What people wanted was a flattering picture, the flattery consisting at first not so much in the likeness as in the photographer's accessories.

Most studio furnishings were supplied by one or two wholesale firms specialising in this line, and this had the effect of robbing the portraits of their last vestige of individuality. In his eagerness to pander to the taste of his clients the photographer called in the assistance of the scene-painter, until in the end everything in the studio was make-believe, and the man behind the camera would be more aptly described as a fake-artist and stage-manager than as a photographer. He could change the scenery as required, from an elegant drawing-room with classical pillars and a painted french window framing a lovely view

---

[1] From "The New School of Portrait Painting", *George Cruikshank's Omnibus*.

on to an Italianate terrace, to a country scene with a "genuine" stile but painted trees, or a mountain with cardboard rocks and sham waterfalls.

What could be more preposterous than a lady in evening dress quietly seated in a luxurious easy chair in the middle of a mountain pass, with a roaring cataract rushing madly down within a couple of inches of her immaculate gown—while in consideration of her thin shoes the mountain path is, of course, carefully carpeted?

Middle-aged men appear to spend their lives leaning against a Corinthian pillar as if needing support, with a heavy curtain flapping about their legs; or precariously seated on a balustrade, walking-stick and top hat in hand, oblivious of the magnificent view behind them.

In short, it was forgotten that individuality is expressed as much by the figure as by the features. With how much more character can a portrait be endowed when the subject is in a position natural to him, than if forced into one to which he is unaccustomed! Yet such was the trend of fashion that people were frequently represented in positions, and in surroundings, vastly unlike those in which their friends usually saw them.

The *carte* picture of women is in the nature of a small fashion-plate. The sitter is usually represented full-length to show off her latest dress and to do justice to the photographer's elegant interior decoration. As in all fashion-plates, head and body are only pegs on which to hang clothes. Facial expression is a secondary consideration since only a tiny representation of the head appears in the picture. The fashion for the *carte-de-visite* considerably lightened the photographer's task. All his skill in flattery was directed towards the arrangement of the pose and his stagy interior.

Absurd flattery achieved by retouching the negative became the chief characteristic of the larger photographic portraits, for which a demand gradually arose in the same proportion as the craze for the *carte-de-visite* began to fall off about 1866-67.

THE PAINTER-PHOTOGRAPHER

The portrait photographer had almost completely supplanted the miniature painter, and all but the front-rank portrait painters. It was a gradual but quite marked evolution, and not without serious

11

repercussions upon portrait photography. Sitters had always expected an idealised portrait, and naturally the photographer had to adjust his art to the practice which had been adopted by portrait painters, with few exceptions, for centuries. Vanity is inherent in human nature, and since it was often objected that the camera represented the countenance too truthfully, the photographer had to interpret his duties more widely than he may have wished. In this respect he was placed in the same dilemma as the fashionable portrait painter, and as only a few had the moral courage to follow their artistic conscience, it became general practice to remove defects and add points of beauty lacking in nature, by retouching. Whilst it may be legitimate to suppress defects by skilful posing and lighting, actual beautifying can only be done by interfering with the negative or painting on the print, and in doing this the photographer leaves his proper domain of drawing with light and becomes that unwholesome hybrid the painter-photographer, which race, though steadily declining in numbers, has not yet died out.

The colouring of photographs was patented by the daguerreotypist Richard Beard in 1842. From that time on, those who believed in photography as an independent art-medium argued that photographs must be produced solely by the action of light on sensitive materials, and that any manual interference more or less obliterated the photographic quality, and so was against the interests of the art. In the late 1850's retouching was carried to such extremes that photographic societies banned coloured photographs altogether from their exhibition walls, and in the case of touched-up photographs often stipulated that the negative should be exhibited alongside the print. Indeed, the ease with which anyone with a little artistic skill could add to or take away from the negative presented a dangerous temptation to photographers in their attempts to flatter the sitter and to achieve "artistic effects".

"The colorist may correct with his brush defects which, if allowed to remain, spoil any picture. For instance, where a head is so irregular in form as to become unsightly, soften those features which are the most strikingly deformed, and reduce the head to a greater semblance of beauty. Try to discover what good points there are—for all heads have some good points—and give these their full value."[1] In his aspira-

---

[1] *Photographic News*, 3rd June 1859, p. 149.

tions towards the Victorian ideal, the photographer would try to make his sitter's features conform to some such description as the following;[1] with what result, may be left to the imagination of the reader:

[*For women*] A handsome face is of an oval shape, both front view and in profile. The nose slightly prominent in the centre, with small, well-rounded end, fine nostrils; small, full, projecting lips, the upper one short and curved upwards in the centre, the lower one slightly hanging down in the centre, both turned up a little at the corners, and receding inside; chin round and small; very small, low cheek-bones, not perceptibly rising above the general rotundity. Eyes large, inclined upwards at the inner angles, downwards at outer angles; upper eyelids long, sloping beyond the white of the eye towards the temples. Eyebrows arched, forehead round, smooth and small; hair rather profuse. Of all things, do not draw the hair over the forehead if well formed, but rather up and away. See the Venus de Medici, and for comparison see also Canova's Venus, in which latter the hair is too broad.

[*For men*] An intellectual head has the forehead and chin projecting, the high facial angle presenting nearly a straight line; bottom lip projecting a little; eyebrows rather near together and low (raised eyebrows indicate weakness). Broad forehead, overhanging eyelids, sometimes cutting across the iris to the pupil.

THE HIGH PRIESTS OF PHOTOGRAPHIC ART

The more intelligent photographers, seeking an escape from the mass production of portraits of the kind described, consoled themselves by making pictures after their own heart in their spare time, which they sent to exhibitions in the hope of redeeming their honour, and to defend the right of photography to be classed as art. The intention was praiseworthy, but the new attempt to rival painting was ill-conceived. Most prominent amongst this group of professionals were O. G. Rejlander and H. P. Robinson, whose work must be briefly mentioned because Lewis Carroll was considerably influenced by the former, and was at least in contact with the latter.

Oscar Gustave Rejlander was a Swede by birth, who studied painting in Rome, where he supported himself chiefly by copying Old Masters. Drawn to England by a love affair, he settled here and set up as a

---

[1] *Ibid.*, 20th May 1859, p. 125.

13

portrait painter. In 1853 he took lessons in photography with the idea of making photographic studies of models as an aid to his painting. It was only in 1855 that Rejlander opened a *photographic* portrait studio in Wolverhampton. Five years later he moved to London, and there continued to practise as a professional photographer until his death in 1875.

Rejlander achieved immortality in the annals of photography with a huge composition picture, printed from over thirty negatives, entitled, at first, "Hope in Repentance" and later "The Two Ways of Life". It was somewhat reminiscent of the *tableaux vivants* which the Victorians were so fond of arranging. The religious and moralising content of the picture attracted Queen Victoria's attention when it was first exhibited at the Manchester Art Treasures Exhibition in 1857, and she bought it. For many years, heated discussions took place in photographic circles over the suitability of treating such subjects photographically and the propriety of combining a number of negatives to make one picture.

Rejlander delighted in composing pictures that tell a story, and followed up "The Two Ways of Life" with other composition pictures, though nothing on so large a scale, nor of quite so controversial a nature.

He also made studies for artists to work from—nudes, drapery, close-ups of hands and feet. His photographs of little children attracted Lewis Carroll, and, some years later, Charles Darwin, whose book *The Expression of the Emotions in Man and Animals* Rejlander illustrated. Lewis Carroll mentions Rejlander several times in his diaries. He sat to him for his portrait [Plate 1], and also collected his photographs (see album X, p. 102).

Henry Peach Robinson was also an art student before he started as an amateur photographer in 1852. Five years later he opened a professional portrait studio in Leamington Spa. In 1866 the studio was transferred to London, and after another two years he took into partnership N. K. Cherrill and they started an establishment at Tunbridge Wells, where Robinson remained in business for the next twenty years.

As an artist, H. P. Robinson's main interest lay in composition pictures, in which he surpassed Rejlander. His first and most famous picture, "Fading Away", was shown at an exhibition of the Photo-

14

graphic Society in London in 1858. From then on, Robinson resolved to produce a new composition every year. They were usually of large size, mostly rustic scenes, or interiors, in which the principal interest was centred in the figures. These productions raised Robinson's status, though in retrospect it is doubtful whether they did honour to the art by which he lived.

Lewis Carroll–Photographer

LEWIS Carroll's photography extends over a period of twenty-four years—from May 1856 until July 1880. His diaries disclose a devotion to his hobby which goes beyond all expectation. Although only brief, factual notes, the entries do reveal to what an extent photography affected him personally, and the part it played in his relationship with his child friends. In some years there are almost daily entries, so that one wonders how the Oxford don ever found time for his duties as mathematical lecturer, his countless friendships with children, his voluminous correspondence, his frequent visits to London theatres, and, above all, his prolific writing, including the masterpieces *Alice's Adventures in Wonderland* and *Through the Looking-Glass and What Alice Found There*, both of which were written during the period of Lewis Carroll's photographic activity. The years 1863 and 1864 particularly have more frequent and longer entries than any other years, and may be regarded as the most important period. It will be seen from the illustrations that many of his best pictures were created at this time.

Portraiture was Lewis Carroll's main field, though he also took a few landscapes, photographed sculpture and skeletons, and amused himself by reproducing a curious assortment of prints and drawings. It is only in portraiture that he uses the camera as something more than a mere recording machine, that the creative element enters his work, and a definite style manifests itself in his choice and treatment of subject, which is immediately apparent to anyone who studies a representative collection of his photographs. Impressed with his personality, the portraits demand attention from the artistic no less than from the human point of view, and in examining them we discover in the man behind the camera characteristics which we have not met in the Rev. C. L. Dodgson nor in Lewis Carroll the author.

LEWIS CARROLL'S SITTERS

Apart from some early photographs of his family and of members of Christ Church Common Room, Lewis Carroll's portraits fall into two clearly defined categories—distinguished people, and children.

His hobby reveals him as an indefatigable lion-hunter—which is the more surprising since Lewis Carroll strongly resented being lionised himself. At first it may seem difficult to reconcile this trait with his well-known shyness and reserved manner, but it is only one of the many contradictions in his character. The effort it must have cost him to overcome this shyness in his determination to track down eminent men and women is a measure of his keenness on photography.

In considering his portrait work as a whole, the photographs of children are of infinitely greater artistic interest than the portraits of the famous, and we feel sure that the enchanting picture of Beatrice Henley [Plate 14] and her sprawling signature in his album meant more to Lewis Carroll than the dull portrait of the Crown Prince of Denmark [Plate 35], in spite of the imposing autograph beneath it.

With children Lewis Carroll was far more at ease than with grown-ups, in whose society his manner is said to have been "almost old-maidishly prim". The shy, pedantic mathematical lecturer completely unbent in the company of little girls, whom he never tired of entertaining. He loved their childish prattle, and they adored the fantastic stories he invented for them. He himself said that children were three-fourths of his life, and that in their company his brain enjoyed a rest which was startlingly recuperative. To play with children was a tonic to his whole system, and his delightful letters to them reveal childhood surviving in the man of genius.

16

Throughout his life Lewis Carroll looked back on his childhood with longing, and this nostalgia is a recurring theme in his writing. At the age of twenty-one he expressed this emotion in "Solitude":

> Ye golden hours of Life's young spring,
> Of innocence, of love and truth!
> Bright, beyond all imagining,
> Thou fairy-dream of youth!
>
> I'd give all wealth that years have piled,
> The slow result of Life's decay,
> To be once more a little child
> For one bright summer-day.

He reverted to the same theme at the age of forty-four in *The Hunting of the Snark* (Fit the Fifth):

> He thought of his childhood, left far behind—
> That blissful and innocent state.

and again seven years before he died, in "Puck Found".

> All too soon will Childhood gay
> Realize Life's sober sadness,
> Let's be merry while we may,
> Innocent and happy Fay!
> Elves were made for gladness!

We can think of no better illustration of Lewis Carroll's merrymaking in the company of children than the amusing account[1] Sir George Baden-Powell gives of his first introduction to the author of *Alice in Wonderland* about 1870 or 1871.

> I was then coaching at Oxford with the well-known Rev. E. Hatch, and was on friendly terms with his bright and pretty children. Entering his house one day, and facing the dining-room, I heard mysterious noises under the table, and saw the cloth move as if some one were hiding. Children's legs revealed it as no burglar, and there was nothing for it but to crawl upon them, roaring as a lion. Bursting in upon them in their stronghold under the table, I was met by the staid but amused gaze of a reverend gentleman. Frequently afterwards did I see and hear "Lewis Carroll" entertaining the youngsters in his inimitable way.

---

[1] Stuart Dodgson Collingwood, *Life and Letters of Lewis Carroll*, 1898, p. 344.

Just as the *Alice* books, and indeed most of Lewis Carroll's finest literary work, were inspired by his little girl friends and are dedicated to them, so also were these friends the inspiration of his most charming photographs.

Beautiful little girls had a strange fascination for Lewis Carroll. This curious relationship, which may best be described as innocent love, ceased in the majority of cases when the girls put up their hair. "About nine out of ten, I think, of my child friendships get shipwrecked at the critical point 'where the stream and river meet', and the child friends, once so affectionate, become uninteresting acquaintances whom I have no wish to set eyes on again."

The majority of the little girls illustrated in this book were the daughters of clergymen, of Oxford professors, of well-known writers and artists. While the Rev. C. L. Dodgson undoubtedly believed in the equality of all souls before God, he also believed, like all other Victorians, that the classes should keep to themselves. A streak of snobbery occasionally comes to the surface, as, for instance, in the hitherto unpublished letter to Beatrice Hatch (page 82). All the same, the charming picture of the lodge-keeper's niece [Plate 43] shows that he had no hard-and-fast rules so far as his hobby was concerned, provided the little sitter was attractive.

With boys Lewis Carroll was out of his element. He summed up his feelings about them in an unintentional *bon mot*: "I am fond of children, except boys." "To me they are not an attractive race of beings," he wrote to a school-mistress, "and if you wanted to induce me by money to come and teach them, I can only say you would have to offer more than £10,000 a year." An Oxford friend who suggested bringing round his little boy on a visit could hardly believe his eyes when he received a note from Lewis Carroll saying "Don't", or words to that effect. "He thought I doted on *all* children, but I am *not* omnivorous like a pig. I pick and choose." Boys, therefore, he photographed only when they were pretty in a girlish way, when they were brothers of his girl friends and could not very well be left out, or, occasionally, when they could be used as a bait to catch their famous parents.

In his constant desire to meet children, Lewis Carroll pressed his friends for introductions to families with good-looking daughters— though by no means all his friendships started in this conventional way.

He went to archery meetings and Freemasons' fêtes to find subjects and was always ready with stories and games to amuse little girls whom he met on a journey, in a park, and, above all, at the seaside, where he habitually spent part of the Long Vacation because the beach afforded especially good opportunities for such chance encounters. Lewis Carroll delighted in watching children at play, would make them paper boats or show them puzzles, and always came to the rescue with safety-pins if he saw a little girl hesitating to paddle in the sea for fear of spoiling her frock. When he had won the parents' confidence by presenting the child with a copy of *Alice* "From the Author", such acquaintanceships often ripened into friendships.

Lastly we have to make a passing reference to Lewis Carroll's many friends amongst actresses. He was a keen theatre-goer and his admiration for Kate and Ellen Terry [Plate 47] led eventually to an intimate friendship with the whole Terry family, each member of which he photographed. Frequent visits with children to the pantomime, and the opportunities afforded at rehearsals of the dramatised versions of the *Alice* books, resulted in many friendships with child actresses in the 1880's and 1890's, but these he took to professional photographers for their portrait, having given up his hobby in 1880.

PHOTOGRAPHING CHILDREN

Lewis Carroll's gift for entertaining children, which was to play such an important part in his photography, was already highly developed during his own childhood. At Croft Rectory, Yorkshire, he found plenty of opportunity for inventing amusements for his seven sisters and three brothers. He improvised a "railway", built a marionette theatre, performed conjuring tricks, and produced a succession of family magazines. At Christ Church the usually staid don relaxed in the company of little visitors to his large suite of rooms—a veritable children's paradise. There was a wonderful array of dolls and toys, a distorting mirror, a clockwork bear, and a flying bat made by him. This latter was the cause of much embarrassment when, on a hot summer afternoon, after circling the room several times, it suddenly flew out of the window and landed on a tea-tray which a college servant was just carrying across Tom Quad. Startled by this strange apparition, he dropped the tray with a great clatter. Of course, it did not take long before he realised what had happened, for Dodgson's eccentricities were a well-known feature of life at Christ Church.

Musical entertainment was provided by a collection of twenty or so musical boxes, and an organette in which he would sometimes insert the perforated music sheet backwards so as to puzzle his young friends, just as he delighted in sending them letters in mirror-writing.

When the novelty of these attractions began to pall, Lewis Carroll would take a child on his knee and tell her fascinating tales, illustrating them with comic drawings on scraps of paper. When she was thoroughly happy and amused by his stories, he would pose her for a photograph before the right mood had passed. "Being photographed was a joy to us and not a penance, as it is to most children," related Mrs. Reginald Hargreaves (the former Alice Liddell), whilst Miss Evelyn Hatch, another child friend, looks back on Lewis Carroll's photography with rather mixed feelings. "Opinions were somewhat divided as to whether it were really a great treat. It meant much patience, for the photographer was always determined to get his picture 'just right'."

Sometimes Lewis Carroll enjoyed posing his little sitters in fancy dress. He had a cupboard full of costumes: some had been used in pantomimes at Drury Lane, some had been borrowed from friends or, on occasion, even from the Ashmolean Museum; others were mere rags to pose them as beggar-children. As early as 1857 he dressed up a little girl as "Little Red Riding-hood", but it is not until many years later, chiefly in the 1870's, that we find this outburst of costume pictures—"Chinamen", "Turks", "Greeks", "Romans", "Danes", and a whole string of "Beggar-girls" and "Dolly Vardens".

Apart from those illustrated in this book, there are Kate Terry as "Andromeda", Rose Wood in the character of "Jeannie Campbell", Xie Kitchin dressed as Reynolds's "Penelope Boothby", Holman Hunt's little nephew as "the King of Hearts", Q. F. Twiss, an undergraduate at Christ Church, as Dickens's "Artful Dodger" and other characters, and a horrible "nun".

It goes without saying that most of these costume pictures have to be condemned as errors of taste. Whereas Lewis Carroll's other photographic work shows a remarkable independence of contemporary photography, the sentiment of these pictures is a lamentable concession to Victorian taste. As a producer of costume pictures Lewis Carroll is almost always banal; as a photographer of children he achieves an excellence which in its way can find no peer.

Among the few successful costume pictures we would count Ellen Terry [Plate 47], Wicliffe Taylor as a knight [Plate 18], "St. George and the Dragon", and the study of Irene MacDonald entitled "It Won't Come Smooth" [Plate 16]—a real gem. This last, though, is "undressing" rather than "dressing up"! Lewis Carroll considered children's simple nightdresses most becoming, and quite a number of little girls were posed in them. He wrote to a mother, "If they have such things as flannel night-gowns, that makes as pretty a dress as you can desire. White does pretty well, but nothing like flannel"—the texture and colour of which are more photogenic than white cotton. In a letter to Harry Furniss, illustrator of *Sylvie and Bruno*, about dresses for the fairy children he goes a step further: "I *wish* I dared dispense with *all* costume. Naked children are so perfectly pure and lovely; but Mrs. Grundy would be furious—it would never do."

Characteristically, his dislike of boys extended also to their nakedness. "I confess I do *not* admire naked boys. They always seem to me to need clothes—whereas one hardly sees why the lovely forms of girls should *ever* be covered up."

In his hobby there was no danger of outraging Mrs. Grundy provided he found little girls—and parents—who raised no objection. Lewis Carroll showed great consideration for the susceptibility of his young sitters, believing that if a girl had any scruple on the score of modesty, such feelings ought to be treated with the "utmost reverence". A letter to Miss Gertrude Thomson, another of his illustrators, demonstrates his delicacy in this matter. "If I had the loveliest child in the world, to draw or photograph, and found she had a modest shrinking (however slight, and however easily overcome) from being taken nude, I should feel it was a solemn duty owed to God to drop the request *altogether*."

If Lewis Carroll's photographs of nude girls were as sentimental and devoid of artistry as Miss Thomson's drawings of fairies in *Three Sunsets*, we must be grateful to him for having stipulated that after his death they should be returned to the sitters or their parents, or else be destroyed. Naturally none of them were pasted in his albums, and as far as I know, none have survived.

21

Another aberration in taste was his admiration for the productions of "artist photographers" such as H. P. Robinson, O. G. Rejlander and Lake Price, who in their zeal to raise photography to the status of high art produced a long succession of "imitation paintings"—elaborate compositions on historico-romantic and anecdotal themes such as were particularly beloved by Victorian Academicians, Mulready, Leslie, Augustus Egg and others. If their canvases seem poor to us, *photographic* story-telling is quite ludicrous, on account of the limitations inherent in the photographic medium; yet so ingrained was the Victorian love for this type of subject that even photography—a medium whose sole contribution to art lies in its inimitable realism—was employed to illustrate historical reconstructions and imaginary themes.

Of Lewis Carroll's own efforts in anecdotal composition we would mention only two, which may enable the reader to form his own opinion: "The Elopement"—rather a surprising choice of subject for a clergyman—anticipates a Hollywood film shot [Plate 15]; "The Soldier's Farewell" depicts a youth in volunteer uniform embracing a young girl, who weeps on his shoulder.

THE GLASS-HOUSE

Many of Lewis Carroll's photographs were taken in Oxford—either at the Deanery, Christ Church, or in his rooms, or in a hired studio. When, in November 1868, Lewis Carroll moved into a fine suite of rooms in the north-west corner of Tom Quad, he sought permission to erect a photographic glass-house on the flat college roof, with direct access from his rooms. Even without requiring a building licence from the Ministry of Health, it seems to have taken a very long time until permission was granted, for it was only in October 1871 that he was able to report the completion of the new studio.

This photographic glass-house was a particular attraction for little visitors during the next eight years.

Perhaps the most vivid memories of the Oxford children are connected with the great experience of being photographed. How well they can remember climbing up the dark oak staircase leading out of Tom Quad to the studio on the top floor of his rooms! The smell of certain chemicals will still bring back a vision of the mysterious dark cupboard where he developed his plates, of the dressing-room where strange costumes had to be donned, and of the rather awe-inspiring ceremony of being posed, with fastidious

22

care, as Turk, Chinaman, fisher-boy, or in a group with several others to form a picture. Boys as well as girls were invited to be photographed, but opinions were somewhat divided as to whether it were really a great treat. It meant much patience, for the photographer was always determined to get his picture "just right", and it must be owned that there is a certain expression of boredom on the faces of some of his young models, who remember that the studio was very hot, and that they used to get very tired of sitting still! Occasionally, as a reward, they were allowed to go out on to the flat roof above, and look at the view of the Oxford towers.[1]

"But much more exciting than being photographed was being allowed to go into the darkroom and watch him develop the large glass plates," related Mrs. Hargreaves,[2] and we can imagine her wonder and delight when the picture slowly unfolded itself as her friend gently rocked the negative to and fro in the developing dish.

Still more excited than the sitters was the photographer himself. "I am taking pictures almost every day," he wrote to Mary MacDonald soon after the studio was finished. "If you come, bring your best theatrical get-up, and I will do you a splendid picture." He remonstrated with Agnes Hull five years later (December 1877), "Oh! child, child! Why have you never been over to Oxford to be photographed? I took a first-rate photograph only a week ago, but then the sitter (a little girl of ten) had to sit for a minute and a half, the light is so weak now. But if you could get anyone to bring you over, I could do one, even now."

TECHNICAL NOTES

The glass-house enabled Lewis Carroll to take photographs in the winter months, a thing which he rarely did before on account of the long exposures required. All the same, a minute and a half is a very long time for a little girl to sit still, even with the support of a head-rest, which Lewis Carroll did not disdain to use occasionally. Naturally, on a really fine day the exposure was considerably shorter; according to a diary entry of 28th October 1876, it was 45 seconds. Incidentally, these are the only references we have as to exposure time, except in

---

[1] Evelyn Hatch, *A Selection from the Letters of Lewis Carroll to his Child Friends*, p. 3.

[2] Capt. Caryl Hargreaves, "Alice's Recollections of Carrollian Days as Told by her Son", *Cornhill Magazine*, July 1932.

"A Photographer's Day Out", when we are informed that it was necessary to give one minute and forty seconds to take a calotype (Talbotype) of a cottage in August.

When Lewis Carroll travelled, which he did a good deal, he usually took the photographic outfit with him, whether staying with friends or relations, or going on holiday. This was no light undertaking; it demanded a passionate devotion to one's hobby, and those with only a casual interest soon dropped out of the game. Apart from camera, lens and tripod, the whole paraphernalia which were such a burden to the travelling photographer in the wet-plate period accompanied him on his photographic tours: a chest full of bottles containing chemicals for coating, developing, fixing and varnishing the glass plates, bottles of various sizes containing stock solutions, a number of dishes, a good stock of glass plates, scales and weights, glass measures and funnels, and, above all, a portable dark tent or cupboard in which all the chemical hocus-pocus took place. The latter—which was shown at the Lewis Carroll Centenary Exhibition in London, 1932—consisted of a shallow box or tray about 21½″ long by 17½″ wide by 4″ deep, the lid forming the top of the tent. Round this tray hung a curtain of yellow calico which wrapped round the operator and excluded the light. The whole was supported on a tripod stand, and could be folded up for transport. The time Lewis Carroll must have spent packing up this outfit—knowing his fastidiousness in packing his personal belongings, wrapping each item separately in paper twice its own bulk—hardly bears thinking of.

Since it was both ungentlemanly and uncomfortable to be bent double beneath the weight of cumbersome apparatus, many photographers engaged a man as a porter. "After all, the portability is only a question of degree; if you carry it yourself it becomes heavy before you have gone half a mile, and if you hire a man to carry it for you, it may just as well be ten pounds heavier," wrote a travelling photographer.[1] Undoubtedly Lewis Carroll did not indulge in such kind sentiments, but neither was he prepared to make himself ridiculous by pushing a photographic wheelbarrow or perambulator, as fell to the lot of many of the photographic fraternity. Wherever he went, he sent the apparatus in

---

[1] *Photographic News*, 29th October 1858, p. 91.

advance by rail, and when in London took it from place to place in a cab.
Wishing to avoid moving the photographic equipment about un-
necessarily, Lewis Carroll often obtained permission to receive sitters,
when he had found a suitable *pied-à-terre*. He was, for instance, immensely
impressed by the great variety of architectural backgrounds at Lambeth
Palace, and forthwith made it his photographic headquarters for three
weeks. On another visit to London it was the picturesque flight of
steps into D. G. Rossetti's garden which caught his eye, and for several
days he happily photographed there whoever was on his list at the time.
Whether Rossetti shared Lewis Carroll's enjoyment is not recorded, but
we cannot help suspecting that the photographer occasionally made
himself a bit of a nuisance, though in his enthusiasm he would have
been quite insensitive to any such reaction.

Some of Lewis Carroll's rules were rather one-sided affairs. We come
across many contradictory traits in his character: he had a horror of
being photographed but never tired of pressing others to sit to him;
he was fond of collecting *cartes* but to have his own portrait collected
by others was distasteful to him; he was a lion-hunter who hated to be
lionised himself; he was a great autograph collector but when he suspected others of writing to him only in order to get his signature he
would use script or a typewriter and ask a friend to sign for him. Caricatures went only one way too, as the incident with Isa Bowman shows.
When Lewis Carroll saw a caricature which she had attempted of him,
he went red in the face, snatched it from her and tore it up. Another
incongruity was that in spite of his dislike of receiving surprise visits he
often dropped in on people unexpectedly himself. Imagine Tom Taylor's
delight when Lewis Carroll arrived in a cab with all his apparatus
about half-past eight one morning, before the family had assembled for
breakfast! Noting this in his diary, Lewis Carroll, without reflection on
the merits or demerits of such an early arrival, continues his factual
reporting: "*I had the cellar as a darkroom and the conservatory as a studio, and
succeeded in getting some very good portraits.*"

Such makeshift arrangements greatly added to the immense difficulties the photographer of the wet collodion period had to contend with—
difficulties which we, in these days of factory-produced roll films and
plates, can only appreciate if we have some knowledge of the complicated manipulations necessary at that time.

Stains of inky blackness on hands and clothes earned for the wet-plate process the appellation of "the black art"; yet these, and the odour of the collodion, were only small annoyances compared with the endless trouble entailed in the process.

Although collodion could be bought ready-made, the polishing of the glass plate to obtain a chemically clean surface, the coating itself, the vagaries of the silver nitrate bath, all demanded extremely skilful manipulation. It is certainly no easy matter to balance an $8'' \times 10''$ glass plate—the largest size Lewis Carroll handled—between the thumb and forefinger of one hand while pouring on the collodion with the other, at the same time gently tilting the plate to make the emulsion flow evenly all over it. The sensitising bath was also fraught with difficulties. Then the necessity of keeping the surface of the sensitive plate wet during the exposure, and of observing scrupulous cleanliness in processing, required great dexterity on the part of the photographer. The slightest knock against anything, and the sticky plate would be covered with thousands of particles of dust which might not even be noticed until an abundance of spots appeared on the print:

Development was carried out by balancing the plate, again in one hand, while carefully pouring the developing solution over it.

It hardly needs stressing that the chance of spoiling a negative was particularly great when such delicate manipulations had to be carried out in a dusty cellar, and it is remarkable that Lewis Carroll's photographs have not suffered in this respect at all, thanks to his extraordinary neatness and fastidious care.

If no accident occurred during the processes of fixing, washing and drying, the plate had still to be varnished to give it sufficient protection before proofs could be printed from it. The negative had to be warmed uniformly all over before a fire "as hot as the back of the hand will bear", and then the varnish had to be poured on and strained off into a bottle, in the same way as the collodion and developing solutions.

Before the photographer could print from his negatives he had to prepare the positive paper: that is to say, if he preferred, as Lewis Carroll did, the warm sepia tone of the silver print to the pale yellow tint of the albumen paper which could be bought ready coated.

The sensitising, toning and fixing of positive prints was a simple operation compared with the production of negatives; nevertheless Lewis

Carroll was not very keen on this part of the process, which, admittedly, is the least interesting, and is downright monotonous when several copies of the same picture are required. For this reason he often had his negatives printed by professional photographers. Those taken in London were printed by Joseph Cundall & Co., a well-known firm of photographers in New Bond Street, who also stored the negatives for him. His Oxford photographs were often printed by a firm of portrait photographers called Hills & Saunders, and especially important or difficult jobs were entrusted to H. P. Robinson's firm at Tunbridge Wells.

From the diaries it is quite clear that Lewis Carroll printed and toned a large number of photographs himself, but it is impossible to say which ones he sent out, and in what proportion. Writing to Agnes Hull, whom he photographed in October 1878, he says: "The negatives are dried and varnished, and all but the two large ones of you shall go to the printer here [Oxford]. Those two I want to send to London to be left somewhere where the Tunbridge Wells printer [H. P. Robinson] can call for them."

Untrimmed prints show that Lewis Carroll worked with five plate sizes, ranging from $8'' \times 10''$ to $3\frac{1}{4}'' \times 4\frac{1}{4}''$. His negatives were never enlarged, and since we learn from the diaries that he bought three cameras (of unspecified size), some of the in-between negative sizes ($6\frac{1}{2}'' \times 8\frac{1}{2}''$, $6\frac{1}{4}'' \times 7\frac{1}{4}''$ and $5'' \times 6''$) must have been obtained by having one of the larger cameras fitted with masks to take smaller plates. This assumption does not, however, exclude the possibility that Lewis Carroll may have bought another camera between May 1858 and May 1862, for which period the diaries have been lost. His list of photographs printed for private circulation towards the end of 1860 or early in 1861 (see page 126) mentions only two negative sizes ($6\frac{1}{4}'' \times 7\frac{1}{4}''$ and $5'' \times 6''$), but we know that the first camera was $8'' \times 10''$, for the Rossetti group [Plate 24] was taken on a plate this size seven months before he bought his second camera.

This first camera was bought in March 1856 from the camera manufacturer T. Ottewill in Caledonian Road, London. On a photographic trip to London in May 1864, Lewis Carroll bought the smallest camera ($3\frac{1}{4}'' \times 4\frac{1}{4}''$) from R. W. Thomas, a chemist in Pall Mall, who also used to supply him with chemicals from time to time. Naturally, the smaller

27

the plate size, the shorter the exposure, and this was of particular importance in photographing fidgety children. All the same, he did not abandon the larger cameras and on several occasions used at least two cameras at one sitting. Even after June 1871, when he bought from Edwin Faulkner, a professional portrait photographer in London, "his camera for taking children quickly", he still sometimes took photographs with the whole-plate ($6\frac{1}{2}'' \times 8\frac{1}{2}''$) camera.

With his meticulous love of order, Lewis Carroll numbered every negative and print, but these numbers unfortunately do not give an exact indication of his total output. A true artist, he would from time to time go through his stock of negatives and erase a good many of them, filling the gaps in the numbers with new negatives, which he prefixed with the sign ℗, meaning "second". In 1875 particularly, he had a thorough clean-up, numbering and cataloguing negatives for a month, often working at it for ten hours a day. Occasionally he also used fractions (e.g. $907\frac{1}{2}$ and $200\frac{2}{3}$), which still further increases our difficulty in arriving at a proper estimate of the number of photographs he took. The highest negative number I have seen—2641, referring to a picture taken the year he gave up his hobby—hardly conveys, therefore, a true idea of the extent of Lewis Carroll's photographic activity.

Apart from some rudimentary instruction in practical manipulation from his uncle, Skeffington Lutwidge, and from Reginald Southey, a fellow Student at Christ Church, Lewis Carroll was more or less self-taught. This fact is in itself not particularly noteworthy. Considering, however, Lewis Carroll's many other activities, his photographic achievements are truly astonishing: he must not only rank as a pioneer of British amateur photography, but I would also unhesitatingly acclaim him as the most outstanding photographer of children in the nineteenth century. After Julia Margaret Cameron he is probably the most distinguished amateur portraitist of the mid-Victorian era.

LEWIS CARROLL AND JULIA MARGARET CAMERON

Lewis Carroll and Mrs. Cameron have many points in common. Both chose portraiture as their main field of activity, and photographed a great many distinguished people; both did their best work in the 1860's and remained, on the whole, uninfluenced by the work of professional photographers. Yet what a world of difference separates their work!

28

For Mrs. Cameron, photography was a "divine art" and she devoted the last fifteen years of her life to its service. Lewis Carroll did not have such high aspirations: photography was his chief hobby during the most important years of his life, but never an end in itself.

Mrs. Cameron was urged on by great ambition, and her work is the expression of an ardent temperament. Lewis Carroll had no ambition; his art springs from delight in the beautiful; he is feminine and light-hearted in his approach to photography, whereas she is masculine and intellectual.

They both despised the absurd characterless productions of most professionals, and dispensed with elaborate, meaningless studio trappings. Yet while Mrs. Cameron cultivated the close-up in the belief that the character and intellectual force of her sitters would stand out more prominently in large head studies, Lewis Carroll, less interested in the intellect of his sitters than in their personality, with few exceptions took full-length portraits, believing quite justifiably that the whole body is much more expressive of what *he* wanted to convey.

Mrs. Cameron progressed beyond that facile characterisation which is a mark of Lewis Carroll's photographs, towards a real exploration of character; her portraits are the creation of a great personality—perhaps the most vigorous and expressive documents we have of the great Victorians. Think only of her striking portraits of Herschel, Tennyson, Carlyle and Darwin, and contrast them with the interesting but quite unimpressive likenesses Lewis Carroll gave us of Faraday, Millais [Plate 48], D. G. Rossetti [Plate 21] and Charlotte Yonge [Plate 57].

The distinguishing feature of Mrs. Cameron's portraits is that she had the real artist's faculty of piercing through the outward appearance to the very soul of the individual. Lewis Carroll did not attempt to plumb the same depths. He did not aim at characterisation, but at an attractive design. With him, the whole arrangement of the picture is expressive: the position of the figure, the placing of accessories, the disposition of the empty space around them, the trimming of the print—everything plays a part, everything is arranged in a decorative manner. He was a master of composition, which was one of Mrs. Cameron's weak points; and though in comparison with her photographs his own take more the form of charming mementoes of a happy hour spent in "loving intimacy" with one of his child friends, the skill and artistry are perhaps too easily overlooked. His portraits of children are both sensitive and immensely personal; they have charm, grace and naturalness—qualities which one seeks in vain in many of Mrs. Cameron's portraits.

The same inherent contrast in their personalities is evident in their technique: Mrs. Cameron was slapdash, Lewis Carroll neat. But though she was less precise, was she not also a more suggestive artist with the camera than Lewis Carroll?

It is interesting to know that the two photographers met on more than one occasion, and to learn Lewis Carroll's opinion of Mrs. Cameron's work. In August 1864, when he was on holiday at Freshwater, Isle of Wight, they spent a happy evening at Mrs. Cameron's house looking at each other's photographs. She had then been photographing for only a few months, but characteristically already spoke of her pictures "as if they were triumphs in art", as Lewis Carroll records with a touch of mockery, adding more critically, "some are very picturesque, some merely hideous. *She* wished she could have had some of *my* subjects to do *out* of focus—and *I* expressed an analogous wish with regard to some of *her* subjects" (i.e. to do them *in* focus).

PHOTOGRAPHIC SOCIETIES

Unlike Mrs. Cameron, and indeed most other prominent amateurs of the period, Lewis Carroll never became a member of the Photographic Society of London, the oldest and most important in the country. The complaints of disgruntled members who aired their grievances about the conduct of the Society in the photographic press cannot have sounded very enticing to prospective members. As the years went by, the Society's meetings, once so stimulating to the new art, deteriorated into feeble debates on uninspiring subjects—the pros and cons of new variations of old processes which were "invented" nearly every week, and other matters of an equally dull and technical nature. Sir William Crookes, the famous scientist, himself a clever amateur photographer, paints in his usual delightfully humorous vein a brilliant picture of the boredom such meetings must have entailed for intelligent members.

This gentleman's speech was interspersed with sundry small (very small) jokes, which relieved the mournful tediousness of the evening and gave some of the least grave among the Members an opportunity of laughing. The discussion was continued for some little time longer in a languid and uninteresting manner, and soon died away altogether; upon which, after renewing the efforts he had several times made during the evening to animate the conversation, the Chairman pronounced the Meeting adjourned.[1]

Lewis Carroll's letters and diaries leave us in no doubt that he delighted in showing his photographs and looking at other people's. There are countless entries referring to his calling on Mr. or Mrs. Blank and leaving his photograph album, or their coming to his rooms to see the latest pictures. Yet in spite of extraordinary devotion to his hobby and pride in his results, he kept aloof from the activities of the Oxford University Photographic Club and the Oxford Literary Photographic Club, both of which were founded some time in the 1870's. He did, however, visit several of the London Society's annual shows, and four of his photographs were hung at the fifth exhibition in 1858—the only occasion on which he exhibited publicly.

RETOUCHING AND COLOURING

Unfortunately Lewis Carroll rarely ventures an opinion on the aesthetics of photography. We only learn that groups were his favourite subject, that he was fond of costume and composition pictures, and that he very much deprecated the prevalent practice of professional photographers of absurdly flattering their sitters by excessive retouching. This latter opinion he held in common with Julia Margaret Cameron, and it was to her son, Henry Herschel Hay Cameron—whom he declared to be the only professional photographer who dared to produce a portrait which was exactly like the original—that Lewis Carroll took Isa Bowman and other girls after he had given up photography himself. The result was *not* appreciated by the little actress, who was Lewis Carroll's chief friend in the late eighties. "I thought that Mr. Cameron's picture made me look a terrible fright, but Lewis Carroll always declared that it was a perfect specimen of portrait work."

Though against retouching to flatter the sitter, he was not above "improving" prints occasionally when the technical quality was not quite up to standard. For instance, he outlined William Michael Rossetti's coat with pen and ink [Plate 24] to make the figure stand out better from

---

[1] *Photographic News*, 8th April 1859, p. 58.

the background; and like the Queen of Hearts' gardeners he painted over white flowers—which had a disturbing effect in the portrait of Tom Taylor [Plate 19]. With the same messy instrument he defined the crown of Lily MacDonald's straw hat [Plate 30].

From drawing on photographs here and there to colouring them all over is not a big step. There are several references in the diaries to having photographs painted in water-colour and in oils by professional artists.[1] It does not seem to have occurred to Lewis Carroll that painting a photograph is not fair to either art. The mind of the artist is cramped by the photograph, and the truth of the photograph is violated by the paint.

Moreover, since retouching and colouring are both abominations which destroy the photographic image, and equally affect the sitter's features, it is clear that Lewis Carroll had no firm convictions on the subject. His objection to retouching did not spring from the belief that such interference is alien to the medium of photography but was obviously *only* directed against flattery.

COMPOSITION

In a collection of portraits made under widely differing conditions—now in the conservatory or garden of a famous man, now in Lewis Carroll's studio, or in the courtyard of a friend's house—there are bound to be occasional slight inequalities in technique, considering the exceptional difficulties under which the travelling photographer of the period laboured. Yet wherever Lewis Carroll was, he took great care that his sitters were perfectly related to their surroundings, and nearly always created remarkably original pictures exhibiting an artistic adventurousness which stands in refreshing contrast to conventional studio portraits.

A glance through any old photograph album will immediately show how much Lewis Carroll's portraits are at variance with the incongruities produced by contemporary professional photographers. There is no forcing of children into the pompous settings so beloved by their

---

[1] In the Author's collection is a coloured photograph of Xie Kitchin as a Chinaman, taken on the same day as Plate 62 but in a slightly different pose. Allowing full play to his imagination, Lewis Carroll had a harbour scene, with sea and Chinese junks, painted in as background.

parents: in his pictures, surroundings and accessories always look natural. Consider the portrait of Coates [Plate 4] which is so simple and yet expresses so much humanity; the wire netting, the weeds growing between the steps, the rough stone walls, are quite daring elements of picture-making for the period—daring, not for their accidental inclusion but for their intentional non-avoidance.

Lewis Carroll shunned backgrounds which would introduce into the picture that restlessness so often apparent in amateur photographs, particularly the patchy light-and-shade effect of foliage in sunshine. Sometimes he would place his sitters in an attractive architectural setting (e.g. Madeline Parnell against a trefoil window at Lambeth Palace, Plate 40) or if that were not available he would choose a wall where a creeper or rambler roses introduced a picturesque note (e.g. Zoë Strong, Plate 26). If there were no suitable background at all, he would ask friends or parents to hold up a blanket (e.g. Aileen Wilson-Todd, Plate 53). This device is not obvious since all his prints are cut down, but I have come across an untrimmed photograph in which the means of support can be seen.

One of the most decorative photographs is probably that of Helene Beyer [Plate 27]. Large patterns usually tend to have a disturbing effect in a photograph, yet here the bold design on Rossetti's screen repeating the pattern of the lace brings a wonderful harmony to the composition.

Always manifesting economy of means, the few accessories Lewis Carroll occasionally chooses—a folding ladder, a flower-pot, a dove, a croquet mallet, even a toy gun—reveal a very personal taste, which is expressed with lightness of touch and never fails to add a decorative note.

In grouping, too, Lewis Carroll is infinitely superior to his contemporaries. When *they* took two or more persons in a picture, it is no uncommon thing to see them standing without any connection whatever with each other, as isolated as figures on a chessboard. How harmonious, in contrast, is the group in the drawing-room at Croft Rectory [Plate 6]! In spite of the fact that one sister looks rather uncomfortably squeezed in, the photograph is full of rhythm and on the whole shows good handling of a difficult subject. Other groups which we would single out for praise are "The Two Alices" [Plate 58], Alexander Munro and his wife [Plate 25], Charlotte Yonge and her mother

33

[Plate 56] and the Rossetti family [Plate 24]. In the latter the steps down into the garden, and the tree in the background, help very much in knitting together a pleasing composition.

Less happy, perhaps, are the few pictures in which a young girl has been posed with her father; but then it must be remembered that such groups were taken for the sake of the daughter—papa is quite obviously only an appendage with which Lewis Carroll would much rather have dispensed. Even with famous sitters, as in the Millais family group, it is not the painter or his wife, but their beautiful little daughter who forms the centre of interest. Not-so-famous parents he seems to have excused himself from taking altogether, whenever possible. A Mrs. Bennie, wife of the rector of Glenfield, wrote to Stuart Dodgson Collingwood: "He has most generously sent us all his books with kind inscriptions to Minnie and Doe, whom he photographed, but would not take Canon Bennie or me. He said he never took portraits of people of more than seventeen years of age until they were seventy." This seems to have been a favourite excuse with photographers at the time, for Mrs. Cameron is reported to have used the same argument with people she did not wish to photograph. And who can blame her and Lewis Carroll for having recourse to subterfuge in seeking the freedom of action so necessary for creative work?

Lewis Carroll's Diary Entries

M o s t of my readers will have asked themselves long ago: What led Lewis Carroll to take up photography? It is a question that naturally comes to mind in discussing his hobby, and the answer can be deduced from the entries in his diaries.

In the summer of 1855 Lewis Carroll's favourite uncle, Skeffington Lutwidge, paid a visit to Croft Rectory, the home of Archdeacon Dodgson. Lewis Carroll always enjoyed his uncle's visits, for Skeffington Lutwidge was of a practical and inventive turn of mind and usually had something interesting to show, which was—to use a typical Victorian phrase—both amusing and instructive. On earlier visits he had acquainted his nephew with the telescope and the microscope, with a little gadget for measuring distances on maps, an embossing stamp for letter paper, and other "novelties". This time photography was his latest enthusiasm. He worked with the calotype process, free from patent restrictions since the previous February, and was obviously still a beginner, for Lewis Carroll entered in his diary on 8th September: *"Uncle S. took several photographs of the church, bridge, etc., but not very successful ones."* Two days afterwards they went on a photographic outing to Richmond, Yorkshire.

The fascinating phenomenon of the gradual development of the latent image fired Lewis Carroll's imagination: a week later he used the idea allegorically in "Photography Extraordinary" (see page 110). In this skit a photographer records the thoughts of a feeble-minded young man. Exposure leaves only a faint image on the prepared paper. Subsequent development reveals a weak story of the "milk-and-water school";

35

further development changes it into the "strong-minded or matter-of-fact" style, and finally turns it into a wildly exaggerated version in which Lewis Carroll parodies early-nineteenth-century German romanticism.

There is no further entry until 16th January 1856, when Lewis Carroll went to the annual exhibition of the Photographic Society of London. *"There is a very beautiful historical picture by Lake Price called 'The Scene in the Tower', taken from life—it is a capital idea for making up pictures."*

Lake Price was a water-colour artist, and one of the first to introduce into photography the idea of building up ambitious composition pictures from several negatives. Unable to give my own opinion because I have never seen the picture in question, I referred to *The Art Journal*, in which Robert Hunt, one of the foremost photographic scientists of the nineteenth century, reviewed the exhibition. Discussing this picture, which has for its subject the murder of the young princes at the instigation of Richard III, he writes: "We doubt the propriety of attempting to rival the historical painter. We believe, indeed, that such pictures as these will have a tendency to lower the appreciation of Art in the eyes of the public, and unfit them for receiving the full impression intended by, or for seeing the beauties of, the artist's production."

This visit to the exhibition gave fresh stimulus to Lewis Carroll's interest in photography, and immediately on returning to Oxford he wrote to his uncle (22nd January 1856) to get him a photographic apparatus *"as I want some other occupation here than mere reading and writing"*.

The year 1855 had been an eventful one for young Charles Dodgson. He began it a poor Student, with no definite expectations, and ended it a master and tutor at Christ Church, with an income of more than £300 a year. Presumably he now felt able to afford the expensive outfit for the collodion process, with which he had meanwhile got acquainted through Reginald Southey, a fellow Student at Christ Church. As I have already explained, the collodion process almost completely superseded the calotype within a short period after its introduction, since the advantages of greater rapidity and reliability, extremely delicate detail, and improved half-tones amply compensated for the difficulty of manipulation.

Perhaps Uncle Skeffington, used to the older process, did not trust himself to choose his nephew's equipment, for we learn that Lewis

36

Carroll and Southey went up to London on 18th March 1856 and ordered apparatus from the camera manufacturer T. Ottewill. "*The camera, with lens, etc., will come to just about £15,*" but this sum did not include all the other paraphernalia which were part and parcel of a photographic outfit in the collodion period.

On 25th April the two amateurs went over to the Deanery, whence they hoped to get a good view of the Cathedral, but two attempts proved failures. They worked with Southey's camera, for Lewis Carroll's was not delivered until 1st May. A week later he procured the chemicals from London, after which he spent the afternoon with Southey photographing. "*He and I each took a portrait of Collyns and, after several failures, he succeeded with my help in getting a good one of himself.*"

10th MAY: *Spent a great part of the day photographing with Southey, or rather looking on. He took Faussett, Hewitt, Harington, myself, etc. As it was so good a day for it, I went over to the Library and called to Harry Liddell from the window, and got him to come over to Southey's room. We had great difficulty in getting him to sit still long enough; he succeeded at last, by placing him in a bright light, in getting a fair profile.*

13th MAY: *Southey spent a long time making up developing fluid etc. for me, so that I am now ready to begin the art.*

15th MAY: *Took several likenesses in the day, but all more or less failures.*

During the next fortnight Lewis Carroll seems to have made great strides in his hobby, though, strange to say, he does not specifically mention his first success. The next entry is on 3rd June: "*Spent the morning at the Deanery, photographing the children.*" These were the children of Dean Liddell. Probably only Harry, Lorina and Alice (then aged four) were old enough to be photographed.

On 19th June we find the photographer at Putney visiting his cousin-by-marriage, Charles Pollock, one of the twenty-four children of the Lord Chief Baron, Sir Frederick Pollock, then President of the Photographic Society of London. Charles Pollock, about the same age as his cousin, was an equally keen amateur photographer. Curiously enough, Lewis Carroll does not report any conversations with these "photographic" relations about their common hobby. He merely mentions that Alice Murdoch [Plate 5] was brought over in the afternoon to be photographed. This picture is of special interest since it is one of the earliest extant by Lewis Carroll. With great care he pasted it in his

ALICE , daughter of C MURDOCH. Esq.

O child ! O new-born denizen
Of life's great city ! on thy head
The glory of the morn is shed,
Like a celestial benison !
Here at the portal thou dost stand,
And with thy little hand
Thou openest the mysterious gate
Into the future's undiscovered land
I see its valves expand,
As at the touch of Fate !
Into those realms of love and hate,

Into that darkness blank and drear,
By some prophetic feeling taught,
I launch the bold, adventurous thought,
Freighted with hope and fear;
As upon subterranean streams,
In caverns unexplored and dark,
Men sometimes launch a fragile bark
Laden with flickering fire,
And watch its swift-receding beams,
Until at length they disappear,
And in the distant dark expire

first album (which, inconsistently, he numbered VI, see page 102). On the opposite page he entered in his neat hand the verses which, admittedly poor, are reproduced above because of their close connection with the photograph.

Only a month after taking up photography Lewis Carroll very enterprisingly set off on a photographic tour for the Long Vacation. First he went home to Croft, where several days were spent taking pictures of friends and relations, among them Mr. Benn [Plate 2]. Here he also began his first photograph album.

In August he moved his equipment to the Lake District, then for a few weeks to Whitby on the East Coast; yet while the frequency of the entries proves the photographer's great enthusiasm for his new hobby, they do not contain any information of interest to us.

Back in Oxford, he notes on 1st November: "*I arranged with the Dean* [Liddell] *to go over some fine day soon and have one more try at the view of the Cathedral and the children's portraits.*"

5th NOVEMBER: *I met Dr. Acland* [the famous anatomist] *today, and he gladly agreed to send over his children to the Deanery to be taken any day I like to appoint.* Lewis Carroll continues the entry with a wise remark with which every photographer will readily agree: "*I have come to the conclusion that it is extravagant to attempt photographs on bad days"*; after several more attempts he finally decided, *"I cannot afford to waste any more time on portraits at such a bad season of the year."* Yet in his New Year's resolution (31st December) he is already looking forward to the resumption of his hobby: *"I hope to make good progress in photography in the Easter Vacation. It is my one recreation and I think it should be done well."*

5th FEBRUARY 1857: *Collyns (of Drayton) tells me that there is a fund belonging to Ch. Ch. at present in Chancery, to be appropriated somehow to the encouragement of Physical Sciences, and that the Chancellor would be willing to make an order on it for any college officer, provided it could be somehow brought under that category. He says that it was suggested in C.R.* [Common Room] *that my cultivating photography might entitle me, as a college tutor, to claim some of it. There seems to have been no claim made on it for a long time: the experiment might be worth trying, if it be not straining the interpretation of the original bequest too far.* No doubt it was, for nothing more is heard of this.

On visiting the Taylor Gallery he is again reminded of the pleasures to come with the fine season. *"I think of asking leave to photograph some of the pictures next spring."* Meanwhile much time is spent in selecting views and prospective sitters.

10th FEBRUARY: *Called on Dr. Heurtley, who took me round the garden to pitch upon a situation for taking a photograph of the Cathedral.*

13th FEBRUARY: *Dined at Dr. Barnes and met Drs. Jacobson and Ogilvie . . . Got Dr. Clarke's and Dr. Jacobson's promises to sit for their photographs, and had a long talk on photography with Thomson* [the Provost of Queen's and himself a photographer]—*a very pleasant evening.*

23rd FEBRUARY: *Made an offer to the Common Room of an album for mounting photographs in, offering myself to mount the ones they already have, as well as such others as may be added hereafter.* The offer was accepted and the album (No. VII) is now in the Library at Christ Church (see page 102).

7th MARCH: *Walking with Shuldham in the meadow we met his cousins, the Norrises.* Of course Lewis Carroll's immediate reaction was, *"I must find an opportunity of taking their photographs."* Following his usual procedure, he sent his photograph album to the Norrises, and when it was returned arranged a date for the sittings.

With the arrival of spring, photography plays an ever-increasing part in the Oxford don's life. On 17th April he notes: *"Arranging books to make more room for photographing.*" A few days later (22nd April) he went to the Exhibition of the British Artists. "*I never saw so many good pictures there. I took hasty sketches on the margin of the catalogue of several of the pictures, chiefly for the arrangement of hands, to help in grouping for photographs.*"

We learn that on 9th May "*I breakfasted this morning with Fowler of Lincoln to meet Thackeray (the author), who delivered his lecture on George III in Oxford last night. I was much pleased with what I saw of him: his manner is simple and unaffected; he shows no anxiety to shine in conversation, though full of fun and anecdote when drawn out. He seemed delighted with the reception he had met with last night: the undergraduates seem to have behaved with most unusual moderation.*" After this short contact with the great novelist, Lewis Carroll at once worked out a plan to secure a sitting from him next time he came to Oxford; a few months later (3rd November) he notes: "*Thackeray (a Fellow of Lincoln) tells me that he asked his cousin (the writer) to give me a sitting for a picture, when he was in Oxford the other day. He consented to come, but had not time then.*"

Meanwhile, on 26th May Dr. Acland showed Lewis Carroll the skeleton of his tunny-fish in the Anatomy Schools, of which he wanted to have pictures taken. In his enthusiasm the photographer, who had not yet discovered his predilection for children, took in his stride everything that came, and subsequently produced a whole series of photographs of skeletons.

29th MAY: *Went to the Deanery about 12 o'clock. I lunched at the children's dinner, and worked hard at photographs all the rest of the time till past 4; it was a very pleasant day on the whole, tho' not successful in photography.*

2nd JUNE: *Spent the morning at the Deanery. Harry was away, but the two dear little girls, Ina and Alice, were with me all the morning. To try the lens, I took a picture of myself, for which Ina took off the cap, and of course considered it all her doing!*

Southey came for a short time in the afternoon to help in the pictures, and before 5 I had got everything packed up, and returned with the camera. The author acquired from Miss F. Menella Dodgson several negatives of self-portraits of Lewis Carroll taken at different periods of his life, and no doubt obtained in a similar way. They bear his negative numbers, and show him seated in his black leather-covered armchair or on his settee,

40

which proves that they are his own and not the negatives of other photographers taken in *their* studios.

9th JUNE: *I breakfasted with Marshall to meet Cotton, a Senior Student. He photographs on paper* [calotype] *and is going to present Common Room with his pictures. He wanted me to join in a photographic tour in France, where he means to live out in the fields in a tent*—but love of his hobby did not go so far as to induce Lewis Carroll to agree to such a preposterous idea as camping out, and his remark *"I do not much fancy the plan"* strikes us as a considerable understatement of his reaction.

15th JUNE: *Twiss* [an undergraduate, and a keen amateur actor] *called to ask me to his "Harmonic" this evening, and I took the opportunity of taking his picture, simply, and in a sailor's costume. I intend trying these at Ryman's* [fine-art dealers in the High Street] *as well as the anatomical* [skeleton] *pictures, to see if I can in any way make photography pay its own expenses. Accordingly I took copies of them to the "Harmonic", having written notices underneath that copies may be had at Ryman's.*

Next day there were already twenty-five orders for Twiss's portrait. The idea of making photography pay its way seems to have prompted Lewis Carroll occasionally to sell a negative, or at least its copyright. Two instances have so far come to my notice. The photograph of Tennyson [Plate 8] was published by Joseph Cundall & Co. of Bond Street, London, under *their* name as a *carte-de-visite* on 15th April 1861. Similarly the portrait of D. G. Rossetti [Plate 21] was issued by the London Stereoscopic Co. as a *carte* as well as a cabinet-size photograph.

26th JUNE: *Spent the day (from 10½ to 5) at the Deanery, photographing with very slender success.*

More than ever determined to get good pictures of the Dean and his children before leaving Oxford for the "Long", he photographed up to the last moment, and when the pictures still failed, even delayed the journey.

29th JUNE: *In order to be able to do some photographs in the morning and leave in the afternoon, I resolved on beginning work as early as possible. I went to sleep on the sofa about 9 and woke at 3: from which time till 2 I was packing and photographing alternately without intermission. I then called at the Deanery to report some success, and stayed luncheon. The Dean afterwards came over, but the picture proved inferior. Nearly in despair, but resolved on trying once more in the morning.*

41

30th June: *Photographing and packing all the morning. Mrs. Liddell brought over the children about* 12: *all the pictures failed.*

July and August were again spent at Croft, principally photographing.

18th August: *A party came down from the Castle to be photographed, consisting of* ——, *Mrs. Weld and her little girl Agnes Grace, the last being the principal object. Her face is very striking and attractive and will certainly make a beautiful photograph* [Plate 10; see also Plate 13]. *I think of sending a print of her through Mrs. Weld, for Tennyson's acceptance.* This he did, and soon heard from Mrs. Weld (Tennyson's sister-in-law) that the Poet Laureate pronounced the portrait "indeed a gem".

Arriving at Ambleside in the Lake District on 18th September, Lewis Carroll found that one of the cases with his photographic equipment had been left behind. *"I could not photograph. I therefore walked . . . intending at least to see Tent Lodge (Coniston)* [where Tennyson was staying], *if not to call. When I had reached it at last I made up my mind to take the liberty of calling. Only Mrs. Tennyson was at home, and I sent in my card, adding underneath the name in pencil: 'Artist of "Agnes Grace" and "Little Red Riding-hood" '. On the strength of this introduction I was most kindly received and spent nearly an hour there. I saw also the two children, Hallam and Lionel, 5 and 3 years old, the most beautiful boys of their age I ever saw. I got leave to take portraits of them, in case I take my camera over to Coniston; she even seemed to think it was not hopeless that Tennyson himself might sit, though I said I would not request it, as he must have refused so many that it is unfair to expect it."*

Hoping against hope, Lewis Carroll left Ambleside on 22nd September for Coniston. *"Walked over to call at Tent Lodge to ask leave to take the children's pictures . . . Brought my books of photographs to be looked at. Mr. and Mrs. Tennyson admired some of them so much that I have strong hopes of ultimately getting a sitting from the poet, though I have not yet ventured to ask for it. He threw out several hints of his wish to learn photography, but seemed to be deterred by a dread of the amount of patience required."*

24th September: *Photographs all failed today—the* [silver nitrate] *bath being wrong.* The next day was again spent photographing. *"This time they succeeded well."*

28th September: *I got pictures of Mr. and Mrs. Tennyson* [the portrait of Tennyson is illustrated in Plate 8], *Hallam* [Plate 9] *and a group of Hallam, Lionel and Mr. Marshall's little girl, Julia.*

42

29th SEPTEMBER: *Went over to the Marshalls* [friends of the Tennysons] *about 11 and spent the day till 4 in photography. I got a beautiful portrait of Hallam, sitting, and a group in the drawing-room of Mr. Tennyson and Hallam, Mr. and Mrs. Marshall and Julia.*

13th NOVEMBER (Oxford): *Finished the poem of "Hiawatha's Photographing"* (see page 113). This poem is more than a delightful burlesque on the kind of photography described in another part of this book. What befell Hiawatha is almost certainly based on experiences which Lewis Carroll himself had at one time or another with sitters who were disappointed with his natural, straightforward portraits, having undoubtedly expected a more flattering picture, such as they were accustomed to receive from professional photographers. It was with the double purpose of avoiding such disappointments, and of showing off the distinguished people who had already sat to him, that Lewis Carroll always used to take at least one of his albums with him on photographic tours.

15th NOVEMBER: *Southey proposes our taking a photographic tour together next summer—a plan which I should enjoy exceedingly.* No mention of camping out this time!

20th DECEMBER: *Called on Southey—chiefly to see his new photographs and to leave five of mine with him for the Photographic Exhibition.*

6th JANUARY 1858: *Finished and entered in photographic album some verses on Little Red Riding-hood. I intend to send them also to Southey, for the Photographic Exhibition Catalogue.*
In February Alexander Munro, the sculptor [Plate 25], visited Dr. and Mrs. Acland. *"By Mrs. Acland's request I took over my photographs to show Mr. Munro . . . he begged I would look in at his studio when next in town. He suggested that I should photograph his bust of Dante, which Dr. Acland has."*
During the Easter Vacation Lewis Carroll went to Ripon, where his father, now a Canon of the Cathedral, resided for three months every year.

29th MARCH: *Called at the Deanery and arranged for the party there coming to-morrow to be photographed—also with Captain Smith to come on Wednesday. Also called on the Maisters at Littlethorpe to ask the Miss Maisters to bring over Kathleen Tidy to-morrow, as I want to secure getting at least one good picture while the things are in proper working order.* The silver nitrate bath was a constant source of trouble to photographers, and not infrequently despairing entries appear such as *"Spent the day in attempting to photograph, but the chemicals refused to work properly."*

The following day Kathleen came over to be photographed, but whilst the portraits of the Dean and other visitors succeeded, all of Kathleen failed. She was probably a fidgety little lady. Nevertheless, wishing to try his luck once more, Lewis Carroll walked over to Littlethorpe next day and brought the child back with him, but his renewed efforts were of no avail.

On 13th April Lewis Carroll visited the fifth annual exhibition of the Photographic Society of London, at which, as we have seen, he was himself an exhibitor. The catalogue lists four pictures by C. L. Dodgson: (1) Portrait, (2) Group of children from life, (3) "Little Red Riding-hood", (4) Portrait of a child. *"There are many very beautiful things there, but very little done in grouping—my favourite branch of the subject."*

Three days later Lewis Carroll called on Alexander Munro, who showed him over his studio, *"containing among many half-finished designs, four statues which are going to the Academy to-morrow. He has a large collection of photographs, many from his own sculpture; one he gave me, a duplicate of an exquisite picture by* [H.P.] *Robinson in the Photo. Exhibition this year—it is called 'Juliet' and is an imitation (taken from the life) of Leslie's picture. He gave me carte-blanche to photograph anything and everything in his studio when I come to town in June, whether he is there or not. It is a tempting inducement to take my camera there, especially if (as he seemed to think not unlikely) there is any chance of getting a sitting from the original of 'Juliet' "*.

The diaries from May 1858 to May 1862 have unfortunately been lost.[1] However, we know[2] that in April 1859 Lewis Carroll went to Freshwater, Isle of Wight, and although he refuted the suggestion of having gone there merely to follow the Poet Laureate to his retreat, he did not miss the opportunity of renewing the acquaintance. He found Tennyson in the garden "mowing his lawn in a wide-awake and spectacles. I had to introduce myself, as he is too short-sighted to recognise people, and when he had finished the bit of mowing he was at, he took me into the

---

[1] See Preface to the Dover Edition.
[2] *Strand Magazine*, May 1901. "A Visit to Tennyson" by C. L. Dodgson—contained in a letter to a cousin.

house to see Mrs. Tennyson . . . Her husband begged that I would drop in for tea that evening, and dine with them next day. He took me over the house to see the pictures, etc. (among which my photographs of the family were hung 'on the line').'' Then they went to the nursery, "where we found the beautiful little Hallam (his son), who remembered me more readily than his father had done". After tea, they adjourned to Tennyson's little smoking-room at the top of the house "where we had about two hours' very interesting talk. . . The next day I went to dinner . . . Tennyson told me that often on going to bed after being engaged on composition he had dreamed long passages of poetry ('You, I suppose', turning to me, 'dream photographs').''

The following day Lewis Carroll showed the photograph album to Mrs. Tennyson and the children, who "insisted on reading out the poetry opposite the pictures, and when they came to their father's portrait (which has for motto, 'The Poet in a golden clime was born, etc.') Lionel puzzled over it for a moment, and then began boldly, 'The Pope!' on which Mrs. Tennyson began laughing, and Tennyson growled out from the other end of the table, 'Hollo! What's this about the Pope?' but no one ventured to explain the allusion."

On 4th June Lewis Carroll wrote to Mrs. Tennyson[1] that he intended to send her a copy of his photograph of Hallam, and possibly also of Hallam and Lionel in the group photograph (both taken at Coniston in September 1857), but wishing to have them coloured by an artist "according to the specimen I showed during my visit" he wondered whether Mrs. Tennyson would mind matching the colour of the hair or sending him a few strands. He thought the colouring of the eyes should cause no difficulty, but the hair should be painted a fraction lighter to allow for the lapse of time since the pictures were taken.

About this period Lewis Carroll stayed at Auckland Castle, where an old family friend, C. T. Longley, then Bishop of Durham, was living. For the amusement of the bishop's daughters and nieces Lewis Carroll wrote during his visit "The Legend of 'Scotland' ", the idea of which was suggested by some marks on the wall of a cellar in a part of the castle which was called "Scotland" because of its remote and chilly situation.

---

[1] Letter in private collection.

This fantastic story displays to the full that love of teasing which was a notable trait in Lewis Carroll's relationship with children. In the first part he accuses them of not learning their lessons, of thumping on the piano ("The tunes were such as noe Man had herde before"), etc. Underlying the part of the "legend" called "The Ladye's History" (see page 118) are, no doubt, some personal experiences. The "certyn Artist having wyth hym a merveillous machine called a 'Chimera'" is none other than the author himself, who teases one of the little girls for being too tall for a successful full-length portrait, and for revenging herself cruelly on the unfortunate artist who omitted head or feet from every picture. (In his diary Lewis Carroll probably entered curtly, "*All the pictures failed*".)

When, in October 1859, the Prince of Wales began his studies at Christ Church, the photographer-don at once angled for a sitting, but his request was not acceded to for "His Royal Highness was tired of having his picture taken". Not accepting the Prince's decision as final, Lewis Carroll took courage and approached him personally when an opportunity presented itself on 12th December of the following year on the occasion of Queen Victoria's and Prince Albert's visit to Oxford with other members of the Royal family. At the Deanery *tableaux vivants* were arranged for the entertainment of the royal guests.

I went a little after half-past eight . . . He [the Prince of Wales] *arrived before nine, and I found an opportunity of reminding General Bruce of his promise to introduce me to the Prince, which he did at the next break in the conversation H.R.H. was holding with Mrs. Fellowes* [Dean Liddell's sister-in-law]. *He shook hands very graciously, and I began with a sort of apology for having been so importunate about the photograph. He said something of the weather being against it, and I asked if the Americans had victimised him much as a sitter; he said they had, but he did not think they had succeeded well, and I told him of the new American process of taking twelve thousand photographs in an hour.*[1] *Edith Liddell coming by at the moment, I remarked on the beautiful tableau which the children might make: he assented, and also said, in answer to my question, that he had seen and admired my photographs of them. I then said that I hoped, as I had missed the photograph, he would at least give me his autograph in my album, which he promised to do. Thinking I had better bring the talk to an end, I concluded by saying that, if he would like copies of any of my photographs, I should feel honoured by his accepting them; he*

---

[1] A mechanical copying apparatus by means of which 12,000 positives could be printed from one negative in about an hour.

thanked me for this, and I then drew back, as he did not seem inclined to pursue the conversation.

This humiliating experience makes painful reading. It is certainly a frank admission of lion-hunting an unwilling victim, and we doubt whether the achievement of *any* objective would have been worth the embarrassment. Three days later the Prince gave the promised auto-graph[1]—"Albert Edward P., Frewen Hall, Oxford, December 15th 1860"—and also chose a dozen or so photographs.

Among Lewis Carroll's earliest publications is a curious pamphlet en-titled "Photographs", enumerating 159 pictures taken before 1861 (see page 126). The purpose of the list is not known, but as the portraits are nearly all of Oxford men, we may venture the opinion that it might have been printed for Ryman's, the art dealers, through whom, as we have seen, Lewis Carroll sold a number of his photographs.

10th JUNE 1862: *Went over to Iffley Rectory* [near Oxford] *to arrange about coming there to photograph—settled that the Rumseys should go over there when I go. Mr. Warburton also wants me to take the four children of his brother from Winchester, and I saw Mrs. Neal's two children there and proposed to take them as well: making eleven in all!*

During June and July Lewis Carroll photographed many children and grown-ups in Oxford and its vicinity. Sometimes they came to his rooms, at other times he took his camera to them.

4th JULY 1862. This day is an historic occasion in the history of English literature, and it will no doubt be of interest to quote the diary entry in its complete form, which was unfortunately not made available to me until after the publication of the first edition.

"Atkinson brought over to my rooms some friends of his, a Mrs. and Miss Peters, of whom I took photographs, and who afterwards looked over my albums and staid [sic] *to lunch. They then went off to the Museum, and Duckworth and I made an expedition* up *the river to Godstow with the 3 Liddells: we had tea on the bank there, and did not reach Ch. Ch. again till ¼ past 8, when we took them on to my rooms to see my collection of micro-photographs, and restored them to the Deanery just before 9."* On the opposite page of his diary Lewis

---

[1] Contained in album No. II, now in the possession of Princeton University, U.S.A. Frewen Hall was the house occupied by Edward VII during his academic residence in Oxford.

Carroll added at a later date, "*On which occasion I told them the fairy-tale of* 'Alice's Adventures Under Ground', *which I undertook to write out for Alice.*"

Most readers will know that the three Liddells concerned were Lorina, Alice and Edith. It is inexplicable why Lewis Carroll's nephew-biographer Stuart Dodgson Collingwood shortened the entry, giving the impression that Lewis Carroll and the three little girls were not accompanied by Canon Duckworth, who did all the hard work, rowing the party up the Isis "all in the golden afternoon." It will also be noticed that Collingwood altered the time of return to Christ Church from $\frac{1}{4}$ past 8 to $\frac{1}{2}$ past 8.

During the following months Lewis Carroll wrote out the tale to please the child he loved, illustrating the manuscript with many pen sketches. When he eventually presented *Alice's Adventures Under Ground* to Alice Liddell, she found herself immortalised in two ways; for to make the present more personal the author had pasted on the last page his portrait of the child who had inspired the story [Plate 12].[1]

Shortly before this book came out, *The Observer* published a letter from a correspondent stating that Lewis Carroll's "All in the golden afternoon" was at variance with the official weather report for Oxford. Thereupon I entered into correspondence with *The Observer*, for according to statements of the various members of the boating party, 4th July 1862 was a fine day. How else could they have undertaken the excursion to Godstow, and have had tea on the bank there? Lewis Carroll's diary entry has been quoted above. Canon Duckworth wrote to a friend on 28th March 1898, "I was 'stroke' of the 'pair' of which he [Lewis Carroll] was 'bow' in the famous voyage from Oxford to Godstow. The quaint story floated over my shoulder to the pretty trio of sisters, daughters of Dean Liddell, on that beautiful summer afternoon in the Long Vacation which is described in the introductory verses to the story."

Further confirmation of the fine weather is given by Alice Liddell (then Mrs. Reginald Hargreaves) in the *St. James's Gazette*, 1st March

---

[1] This oval head-and-shoulders photograph is a detail cut out from a larger picture taken by Lewis Carroll in 1859, when Alice was seven years old. The whole picture was reproduced in *Lilliput*, July 1940.

1898: "I believe the beginning of 'Alice' was told one summer afternoon when the sun was so burning that we had landed in the meadows down the river, deserting the boat to take refuge in the only bit of shade to be found, which was under a new made hayrick. Here from all three came the old petition of 'tell us a story'—and so began the ever-delightful tale."

In contrast, examination of the weather record for Oxford on 4th July 1862 indicates that the day was "cool and rather wet. The amount of rain which fell between 10 a.m. on 4th July and 10 a.m. on 5th measured ·17 inch. According to the weather diary most of the rain appears to have occurred between 2 p.m. on 4th July and 2 a.m. on 5th July."[1]

Miss F. Menella Dodgson, who kindly checked Lewis Carroll's diary entry, informed me that a slip in the date is most unlikely. There is an entry for every day of that week, with the day of the week in brackets. 4th July was given as a Friday, and on reference to an almanac I found this correct.

It is strange that it should have occurred to anyone to doubt the goldenness of the afternoon which three generations have accepted, but unfortunately there seems no way of reconciling Lewis Carroll's diary entry and the weather record, and the matter remains an enigma.

Alice's Adventures Under Ground differs in many respects from *Alice's Adventures in Wonderland*, first published in July 1865. The latter is nearly twice as long, for Lewis Carroll added many fresh ideas, omitting, on the other hand, his pen illustrations in favour of Tenniel's.

Twenty years later, when the tremendous popularity of the fairy-tale continued undiminished, the author, believing that many lovers of *Alice* would like to see it in its original form, approached Mrs. Hargreaves asking her permission to publish a facsimile of the original manuscript. This photo-zincographic facsimile, issued in 1886, is not absolutely identical with the manuscript, for Lewis Carroll omitted from it the photograph of Alice, which necessitated rewriting the last line— "happy summer days"—after which he added "The End" on a slip of paper, which was fastened over the portrait.

---

[1] Information contained in a letter dated 17th January 1950 from the Meteorological Office of the Air Ministry to the Assistant Editor of *The Observer*.

We can only surmise his reasons for not including the photograph in the published facsimile. The manuscript of *Alice's Adventures Under Ground* was essentially personal, inspired by and presented to his "ideal child friend". On the other hand, the published facsimile was impersonal, and the author may not have wanted to limit its appeal to all children by associating it with the photograph of one particular child. Another reason, perhaps the weightier of the two, may have been the fact that the public was by now thoroughly familiar with Tenniel's *Alice*, modelled on Mary Hilton Badcock, who bore no resemblance to Alice Liddell.

It is not surprising, perhaps, that the first manuscript version of the world's most famous book for children should fetch a high price when it was eventually disposed of by Mrs. Hargreaves in a London sale, on 3rd April 1928, but the sum of £15,400 which an American book-dealer, Dr. A. S. W. Rosenbach of Philadelphia, paid for it at Sotheby's is fantastic. It was the highest price ever paid for a manuscript at a public sale in England, and £2,500 more than a first folio Shakespeare. The same year it was re-sold by Dr. Rosenbach to Eldridge R. Johnson of New York, for nearly double the purchase money. Twenty years later, after Mr. Johnson's death, the manuscript was bought by subscription for "only" £12,500 and presented by Dr. Luther Evans, Librarian of Congress and initiator of the scheme, to the British Museum, on 13th November 1948.

But let us return from this digression into business to the much pleasanter theme of Lewis Carroll's photography.

He did not leave Oxford until the beginning of August 1862 when he *"Received from Aunt Caroline* [Lutwidge] *a letter Mrs. Frank Smedley had sent her about the Ellisons of Windsor. (I had applied to Menella Smedley to get me leave to photograph the children, who are said by Mrs. Reed to be very beautiful.) Mrs. Ellison had written to say she was quite willing to have the children photographed, but that they were leaving for Malvern."* Nothing reveals better than this entry by what tortuous ways Lewis Carroll occasionally got his sitters. Delighted at the good news, he immediately packed his photographic outfit and set off in pursuit. To find a suitable studio and darkroom in Malvern was no easy matter. Within four days he moved the equipment three times, but at length was able to report triumphantly,

23rd AUGUST: *Have been photographing the Ellisons daily . . . concluded with a large one of Constance as Red Riding-hood.*

At the beginning of September he again visited his relations the Pollocks at Putney, and photographed Constance and Beatrice Henley, the children of the vicar. Beatrice Henley [Plate 14] is undoubtedly the most graceful subject Lewis Carroll ever had before his lens. Was it *her* blue eyes that enchanted him and inspired the poem "Beatrice"? We do not know for certain, but would like to think so, since there is no mention of another Beatrice between this entry and December 4th when the poem was written.

On 5th September Lewis Carroll went over in a cab from Putney to Uplands, Sheen Common, the home of (Sir) Henry Taylor. Here he spent two days photographing the author of *Philip van Artevelde*, his children and the Irish poet Aubrey de Vere, a relative of the Taylors. "*Took also Ewen Cameron* [a son of Julia Margaret Cameron] *and a little girl of a neighbour, Emily Prescott by name. Finished by copying two photographs they have of Miss Julia Jackson* [a niece of Mrs. Cameron]—*one of them has been exquisitely coloured by Watts.*"

In October Lewis Carroll visited friends at Barmby Moor, Yorkshire. After telling us for the hundreth time "*Photographing most of the day*" he continues:

9th OCTOBER: *Took a composition picture, "The Elopement"* [Plate 15], *Alice* [Jane Donkin] *getting out of her bedroom window, with a rope ladder.*

28th OCTOBER (Oxford): *Called on Mrs. Liddell, to ask leave for the artist at Shrimpton's, who is going to colour my photographs of the children, to call and have a sitting, so as to get good likenesses. She simply evaded the question . . . Called on Mrs. Harington* [whose two little girls had been photographed several times] *for the same purpose. She at once consented.*

An unusual entry occurs on 25th March 1863—a list of 107 names of girls "*photographed or to be photographed*". What makes this entry particularly characteristic is that the girls are grouped under their Christian names, all the Agneses and all the Beatrices etc. together; in many cases the date of birth is given in addition!

On 28th March Lewis Carroll went up to London to the studio of O. G. Rejlander to have his photograph taken [Plate 1]. "*I also looked over a great number of prints and negatives, some of which were very beautiful.*"

51

22nd APRIL: *Called at Badcock's* [a draper's shop in Oxford] *to see if his yard will do for photographing: I think myself it will, but have written to Mr. Rejlander to come over and give advice about it.* It seems that from now on Lewis Carroll, concentrating still more on his hobby, wanted to have a room which he could keep exclusively for this purpose. He rented the place (the yard is only a stone's throw from Christ Church, and is entered from St. Aldate's) and from that time until March 1872, when the specially constructed glass-house over his rooms in Tom Quad was ready, most of the Oxford photographs were taken in Badcock's yard. The term "yard" is misleading; Lewis Carroll hired a room there with wallpaper and skirting-board, carpet, etc., as can be clearly seen in the portrait of the Crown Prince of Denmark [Plate 35].

On 16th June the Prince and Princess of Wales were expected to visit Oxford and great preparations were made for their reception. Like all visiting English royalty, the Prince and his bride were to stay at the Deanery, Christ Church. The day before, Lewis Carroll went over to see the royal suite. Here he noticed a magnificent *carte-de-visite* album, which had originally been made for the maids of honour to give the royal couple. Having a poor opinion of the selection of photographs it contained, *"I offered to fill it from my own albums, which I took over to the Deanery, and had an hour or two of work in transferring the pictures."*

Two of the very few entries which are of a technical nature occur on 18th and 23rd June: *"Took my first photograph this year—it was with Horne and Thornthwaite's collodion and in an iron developer."* Five days later: *"Took two pictures with dry collodion plates, one of the bedstead in the Royal room at the Deanery, and the other of the Deanery and Cathedral—for the latter picture Ina and Alice sat in the window of the Royal chamber, and have come out very well in the picture."*

A great disadvantage of the wet collodion process was that the plates had to be coated immediately before use and exposed dripping wet. In the late fifties and during the sixties, countless processes were devised, in which sticky substances—honey, treacle, raspberry syrup and other culinary ingredients—were used to preserve the collodion in a moist state, so that the plates could be prepared several days beforehand, avoiding in addition the necessity of development immediately after exposure. Although strictly speaking none of the plates coated by any of the preservative substances were dry, the term was used in contrast to the wet manipulation.

31st JUNE [sic] : *Went to the archery meeting to find subjects for photography.* During July the photographer tried his hand at "ghost" pictures, with which he *"succeeded very fairly"*. Like painted photographs, "spirit" photography, which had been introduced as a means of amusement by the eminent scientist Sir David Brewster,[1] was another debasement of the young art, which was very much in vogue at the time. The ghostly appearance was achieved by introducing the apparition—usually a female figure draped in sheets— into a "suitable" group for part of the exposure only.

On 21st July Lewis Carroll called at Alexander Munro's studio in London. The sculptor was always most helpful in introducing him to his circle of friends—chiefly well-known artists. This time he promised to get Arthur Hughes, the painter, and Tom Taylor, the playwright and critic, mentioning that the latter knew the Misses Terry, and spoke very highly of them: no wonder Lewis Carroll at once noted, *"I think I must try to get them also as sitters".*

25th JULY: *Went to Elm Lodge* [Heath Street, Hampstead, where George MacDonald and his family were then living] *and spent the morning in making preparations, and took a few pictures in the afternoon.* There he photographed for several days, and on 31st July concludes with satisfaction: *"I have now done all the MacDonalds, their niece Nelly, Mr. [F. D.] Maurice, and three children whom they brought in, Flora and Mary Rankin, and Margaret Campbell."* One of the pictures depicts Lewis Carroll reclining on the lawn in the garden with four of the MacDonald children and their mother on the extreme left.[2] The uncapping of the lens to make this self-portrait was probably done by George MacDonald or Lily, the eldest daughter. It was certainly *not* effected by pulling a string, as several writers have ingeniously suggested; for although Lewis Carroll was of an inventive turn of mind and such a device would work well for removing the cap, it would be of little help to replace it so as to end the exposure.

After the usual visit to Croft, Lewis Carroll moved his camera to Whit-

[1] Sir David Brewster, *The Stereoscope*, 1856, p. 205.

[2] In all the reproductions I know of this picture, Mrs. MacDonald is trimmed off.

by, where he spent the first half of September photographing various friends, friends of friends, and their children. Among these acquaintances was a Mrs. Read, who was well connected and proved helpful in procuring many sitters for the artist.

7th SEPTEMBER: *Mrs. Read talks of getting me leave to photograph the children of Lord Darnley (her cousin) and of Mrs. Parnell (was a Miss Dawson, maid of honour to the Queen).*

29th SEPTEMBER (London): *Reached Mr. Munro's about seven. All my photographic victims seem to be available but the Terrys, who are acting at Bristol.*

30th SEPTEMBER: *Called with Mr. and Mrs. Munro at Mr. Rossetti's and saw some very lovely pictures . . . he was most hospitable in his offers of the use of house and garden for picture-taking, and I arranged to take my camera there on Monday, have Tuesday for friends, and on Wednesday take him and his mother and sister. Went on to Mr. Holman Hunt . . . his little nephew was in the room* [the original of "The King of Hearts", a child dressed up as Henry VIII]. *I had to leave to go with Mr. and Mrs. Munro to dine with a friend of theirs, a Mr. Watkin, a great railway director.* The dinner had probably been arranged by Munro so that Lewis Carroll could meet a new victim, for the entry ends on a familiar note: "*I arranged before we left that Mrs. Watkin should bring her daughter (Harriet, a nice-looking girl of thirteen) to be photographed to-morrow.*"

1st OCTOBER: *Unpacked the camera* [at Munro's studio, 6 Upper Belgrave Place]. *At twelve arrived the little Henry VIII in full dress to be taken, but there was no open-air place, and the light in the studio was very bad, so that the pictures were but poor . . . Mr. Rossetti came to dine. He proposed getting Robert Browning to come on Wednesday to be photographed.* Nothing more is heard of Browning. Next day Lewis Carroll photographed several pieces of sculpture at Alexander Munro's.

3rd OCTOBER: *Set off for Wandsworth in a fly soon after eight and got there in about half an hour, before they had assembled for breakfast. The party were Mr.* [Tom] *Taylor, his wife and sister, and Wickliffe* [sic], *and Ranie (alias Urania) Gordon. I had the cellar as a dark room and the conservatory as a studio, and succeeded in getting some very good portraits* [Plates 18 & 19].

5th OCTOBER: *Went over again to the Tom Taylors—another attempt was made at a "Knight and Lady" group, which, after a regular "scene" with the*

54

intractable Wickliffe, had to be given up. Took several more pictures, chiefly of the servants, packed up and returned to Mr. Munro's, leaving the camera etc. at Mr. Rossetti's.

6th OCTOBER: *Mr. Tom Taylor came in the morning to bring back the albums which he had kept to look over. Went over to Mr. Rossetti's and began unpacking the camera etc. While I was doing so Miss Christina Rossetti arrived, and Mr. Rossetti introduced me to her. She sat for two pictures, Mr. Rossetti for one* [Plate 21], *and also two friends of his who came in, a Mr. Cayley*[1] *and a Mr. Le Gros* [Alphonse Legros, Plate 22], *an artist. I afterwards looked through a huge volume of drawings, some of which I am to photograph—a great treat.*

I am indebted to Mrs. Rossetti Angeli for pointing out that among the collected letters to and from Dante Gabriel, Christina, and William Rossetti, published by Miss Janet Camp Troxell in *Three Rossettis* (Cambridge, Mass., 1937), is an interesting letter from Christina to Lewis Carroll on the subject of his photographs and her contemplated visit to Oxford.

[1864?]

My dear Mr. Dodgson,

We are not at all uneasy about the Clergy Trading Act, but sincerely obliged for your kind trouble taking agency. I hope my list will prove intelligible. We want, please:—

	Copies
My sister in the rainy group	12
Do. . . . . other group	12
My mother playing at chess with Gabriel	3
The group *not* including my sister	4
My mother in this same	9
Mr. Le Gros	2
Mr. Cayley	1
A large oval of Gabriel seated, holding a wide-awake, nearly or quite full-face	2
Also from my brother's sketches:	
His wife standing. (numbered 91)	3
A lady at work (. . . . . 73)	2

Delightful it would be, that possible visit to Oxford. We contemplate it in a spirit of vague approbation. Stirred up by the kind offer of such a Showman, and by a wish to see the sights of Oxford in general and Gabriel's handiwork in particular; weighed down by family immobility;—we tremble in the balance, though I fear the leaden element preponderates. It is characteristic of us to miss opportunities. A year or two ago I had a chance of seeing Cambridge, and of course missed it.

---

[1] Charles Bagot Cayley was a suitor of Christina Rossetti.

7th OCTOBER: *Spent the day at Mr. Rossetti's photographing—took groups* [Plate 24], *and some single ones, of himself, and his mother* [Plate 23], *two sisters and brother William and also of a very fine curly-headed boy (a model) and of Mr. and Mrs. Munro* [Plate 25].

"It was our aim", wrote Christina Rossetti,[1] "to appear in the full family group of five, but whilst various others succeeded, that particular negative was spoilt by a shower and I possess a solitary print taken from it in which we appear as if splashed by ink."

8th OCTOBER: *Was at work most of the day photographing drawings of Mr. Rossetti's.*

9th OCTOBER: *To Mr. Rossetti's, where I took several photographs of a Mme. Beyer* [Plate 27], *a model of Mr. Munro's and of Mr. Rossetti's. In the afternoon moved over with all my belongings to the MacDonalds.*

10th OCTOBER: *Took photographs of Lily, Mary, Greville, Winifred, Miss Powell and Ronald, and of Mrs. Strong, who came over with four of her childrens* One of them was Zoë [Plate 26].

12th OCTOBER: *Mr. A. Hughes came over to be photographed with his children. Got a splendid picture of him with Agnes* [Plate 32].

14th OCTOBER: *Took a large picture of Mr. MacDonald and Lily* [Plate 30]. *Went to Bond Street in a hansom with Greville to leave the negatives* [at J. Cundall & Co.].

18th NOVEMBER (Oxford): *Kitchin* [the Rev. George William Kitchin] *called about 11½ to say he would bring the Prince* [Frederick of Denmark] *to be photographed at half past twelve: (he had consented some time ago to sit). Went over to Badcock's and had everything ready when they arrived. They staid* [sic] *about half an hour, and I took two negatives of him, a 6 × 5 half-length, and a 10 × 8 full-length. In the intervals he looked over my photographs that are mounted on cards, and he also signed his name in my album, saving as he did so that it was the* first *time he had used his new title. (He is now Crown Prince, the news of the death of the old King having come on Monday.)*

The Rev. G. W. Kitchin's father-in-law was British Consul at Copenhagen, and as a child Mrs. Kitchin used to play with Princess Alexandra, who as Princess of Wales became godmother to Alexandra (Xie) Kitchin. It was partly on account of this friendship, and partly because

---

[1] Mackenzie Bell, *Christina Rossetti: a Biographical and Critical Study*, Boston, 1898.

he was an undergraduate at Christ Church, that the Crown Prince consented to sit for his portrait.

25th JANUARY 1864: *Saw Mr. Tom Taylor: we talked a little about my photographic prospects at Easter, and he begged I would write about a fortnight before coming to town, that he might see if he could get me any sitters.* From there he went to Lady Anna Maria Dawson "*to leave for Mrs. Read a selection of my mounted photographs for her to show to friends. Then to Mr. MacDonald's —saw the commencement of the oil painting of Irene which Mr. Darvall is doing for me.*" This refers to one of Lewis Carroll's photographs, which he had coloured in oils.

1st APRIL: *Called on Tom Taylor, to show him my photograph of the Munros: then on Holman Hunt, to give him photographs of the "King of Hearts", then on Mr. J. Leslie, whose children Mrs. Read has secured for me as subjects.*

1st MAY: *Heard from Mrs. Read, enclosing a letter from Lady A. Stanley* [wife of the Dean of Westminster] *to Lady A. M. Dawson, in which she says that she has shown my photographs to the Queen, and is commanded to say that "Her Majesty admires them very much. They are such as the Prince would have appreciated very highly and taken much pleasure in."*

6th JUNE: [The Rev.] *Barker arrived with his eldest child May, whom I had begged he would bring over to be photographed. Took three pictures of her: one, with him, looks first-rate* [Plate 37].

22nd JUNE (London): *Called on Tom Taylor. He can do nothing for me in the photography line. Thence to Lambeth* [Palace] *and found Fanny and Rosamond* [Longley], *who took me over the place and hunted up a dark room for me.*

23rd JUNE: *Went to the Photographic Exhibition, which was very scanty and poor. I did not admire Mrs. Cameron's large heads, taken out of focus. The best of the life ones were Lady Hawarden's* [another prominent amateur photographer]. *Then to the Deanery, Westminster, where I saw Lady A. Stanley, and had a talk about the photographs she had taken to Windsor.*

24th JUNE: *Called on the Archbishop of York, to ask him to sit for a photograph, but he was out. I went to the bazaar held in the Horticultural Gardens for the benefit of the Female Artists at the Kensington Museum. I saw Lady Hawarden's name as keeping a stall there, and wanted to buy some of her photographs. There was one of which they had no copy, and I gave my name and address that one might be sent. This led to Lord Hawarden's introducing himself to me as an old pupil of my father's, and he introduced me to the Viscountess. She had a studio there, and I decided on bringing some MacDonalds to be photographed by her. Went to the MacDonalds and settled to take Mary and Irene to the bazaar the next morning.*

4th JULY: *Took the* [new] *camera etc. from Thomas' to Lambeth Palace.* Until 21st July Lambeth Palace served as Lewis Carroll's photographic headquarters, to which many friends and acquaintances brought their children to be photographed. We mention only those who are illustrated: Ivo Bligh [Plate 38], Grace Denman [Plate 39], Madeline Parnell [Plate 40], Alice Constance Westmacott [Plate 42] and Maria White [Plate 43]. Last, but not least, he took the host himself, Archbishop Longley [Plate 41]. The photographer had also hoped to obtain Princess Beatrice as a sitter, but in this he was disappointed.

8th JULY: *Heard today from Lady A. Stanley—no sitting to be had of the Princess Beatrice. She does not mention the photographs, from which I conclude that the Queen did not keep any.* This remark is hardly an adequate expression of the disappointment he must have felt, for royalty was very much on Lewis Carroll's mind, as can be seen from the several letters from the Queen to himself which he fabricated for the amusement of his little girl friends. The following is a good example of the kind of letter he always hoped to get but never did. "Buckingham Palace. June 22nd. Dear Mr. Dodgson, I hope you will be able to come to our garden party on Friday afternoon. Yours truly, Victoria R."

13th JULY: *Took three boxes of negatives to Messrs. Cundall's place, and went over all the negatives there, putting some back into their places, and re-numbering others.*

On 14th July, not having received an answer from Mrs. Cameron to his request for an introduction to G. F. Watts, a great friend of hers, Lewis Carroll now called on Tom Taylor with a like request. Finding him out, he called on Alexander Munro, who gave him a note of introduction to Valentine Prinsep, the painter, who in turn obliged with a letter to Watts, *"armed with which I at last found my way to 'Little Holland House'. He* [Watts] *received me most kindly . . . He showed me a large photograph by Mrs. Cameron, of Mrs. Watts* [Ellen Terry] *in 'Choosing', and nearly promised to come, with her, on Saturday, to be photographed."*

Little Holland House, the dower house on Lord Holland's estate, was the home of (Sir) Thoby Prinsep and his wife Sara, a sister of Mrs. Cameron. Many years earlier G. F. Watts had gone to Little Holland House on a three days' visit, but its atmosphere appealed to him so much that he stayed for thirty years! Watts was now the leading portrait painter in Britain, and the above fully discloses by what roundabout ways Lewis Carroll at last contacted the famous man. Fearing that he might not come to Lambeth Palace after all, he proposed in a letter on the following day *"to bring my camera to Little Holland House, and take pictures there of him and his friends: a tolerably cool proposal on my part."*

16th JULY: *Mr. Watts writes to say that he must consult Mr. Prinsep (senior) as to my proposal.* Whereupon he called again at Little Holland House and *"Left for Mr. Watts the photograph I had promised him of Dr. Stanley, to which I added Henry Taylor and Tom Taylor"*. But in spite of these inducements there is no further entry on this subject, which means that Watts declined the offer.

From London, Lewis Carroll went to Freshwater for his summer holiday.

27th JULY: *I noticed in the house* [Plumbly's Hotel, Freshwater] *some photographic machinery belonging to a Colonel Holder, and sent him my card, begging for the acquaintance of "one of the fraternity". He was very friendly, and lent me a portfolio of pictures (all landscapes) which I looked through.*

28th JULY: *Took my photographs into the garden to show to Colonel Holder: his little girl joined us, Helen Agnes, a pretty little thing, whom he has never photographed! Called on Mrs. Cameron, who begged I would bring over my pictures in the evening. Went over to Mrs. Cameron about nine, and found her, two sons and a Mr. Lindsay Neale. Mr. Cameron was unwell. She showed me her pictures, some very beautiful.*

2nd AUGUST: *Went to the Camerons in the evening, and met Mr. Henry Taylor and Mrs. Colonel Franklin (her little girl was one I observed at the school-feast and had enquired her name, with a view to getting Mrs. Cameron to photograph her for me).*

A letter which Lewis Carroll wrote next day to his sister Louisa[1] is more informative about this visit to Mrs. Cameron and his amusing pursuit of Colonel Franklin's little girl.

---

[1] Published here for the first time. Author's collection.

My dear Louisa,

In continuation of my letter to Mary of the 28th, which I suppose contained my history up to the middle of that day, I was asked to go to the Camerons in the evening, and take my photographs—meanwhile I had got into conversation, in the coffee room, with a gentleman and lady (real ones, as my peculiar skill in physiognomy told me) and had exhibited the said photographs to them first: the lady was an artist herself, and took an unmistakable interest in them—it was a real treat to exhibit them to people who so thoroughly entered into them. I saw more of this couple the next morning, when they left, and found they were a Mr. and Mrs. Boyes, of St. James' Terrace, London: we took a great fancy to each other and they "hoped I would call, when in town", do. do. with reference to Oxford. Really I am beginning to think I have the faculty of making friends with people "on the shortest notice".

In the evening Mrs. Cameron and I had a mutual exhibition of photographs. Hers are all taken purposely out of focus—some are very picturesque—some merely hideous—however, she talks of them as if they were triumphs in art. *She* wished she could have had some of *my* subjects to do *out* of focus—and *I* expressed an analogous wish with regard to some of *her* subjects.

The next 2 or 3 days were very enjoyable, tho' very uneventful. I called on Mrs. Cameron on Monday and told her I felt rather tempted to have my camera sent down here, there are so many pretty children about, but that it was too much trouble, and instead, I asked if she would photograph for me (*in* focus) the prettiest two—one being a child of Mr. Bradley's, the master of Marlborough, and the other, name unknown, but constantly to be seen about: I described her as well as I could. "Well then", said Mrs. Cameron, "Next time you see her, just ask her her name." And this I half resolved to do. She also asked me to come in on Tuesday evening, to meet Mr. Henry Taylor, who was coming over from Bournemouth on a visit.

On Monday afternoon I was lounging about on the beach, and came on the same little unknown child—such a little gipsy beauty, rich brown complexion and black eyes.

I was afraid of frightening her if I asked her name, so I came up to the hotel, and got the landlady to come out on to the cliff, who made out for me who she was—a child of the Colonel who commands the fort.

Tuesday evening I went over to the Camerons: Mr. Cameron and Mr. H. Taylor had not yet come up to the drawing-room, and no one was there but Mrs. Cameron and a lady whom she introduced in the usual inarticulate way. I could not catch a syllable of her name, and did not much care. After we had chatted a little, I said "Oh Mrs. Cameron, I have made out who the little girl is I want you to photograph for me. I got the landlady at the inn to make out her name for me. She is Colonel Fonnkland's child."

60

Said Mrs. Cameron, quietly indicating her friend, "*This* lady's child." Wasn't it a curious coincidence (or as Mrs. Cameron called it "a very pretty incident")? Mrs. Franklin (I had got the name wrong) seemed by no means displeased at my wishing for a picture of her child—I showed her some of my photographs in the evening, but Mr. Taylor was anxious to hear her sing, so she had very little time to look at them, and I promised to bring her the rest to her house (which is close by). This I did this morning, and showed them to her, her child Rosa, and her 3 (rather ugly) boys. She is a *very* pleasant and genial person and promises to get Mr. Bradley's children as sitters, as well as her own, if I like to have my camera down here, which I am half tempted to do, as there are many of the peasantry I should like to get also . . .

12th AUGUST: *My camera arrived from London, and I sent it over to Farringford* [Tennyson's home].

13th AUGUST: *Began photographing at Farringford. A long time was spent in getting out things and darkening a room, after which I took three pictures of Annie and three of Colonel Franklin's children.*

15th AUGUST: *With much trouble, I took only two good pictures at Farringford, one a view of the house from the field, and one a large one of Mrs. Franklin and Rose* [Plate 44].

The next day was dull, but in spite of his early decision not to photograph on bad days, he took a picture of the three servants at Farringford, and before leaving Freshwater on the 19th, he did some more "duty" pictures—of the landlord of the hotel and his little boy, and of Tennyson's head man.

20th AUGUST (London): *Took the new negatives to Cundall. Went with Mr. Tom Taylor's note of introduction to* 92 *Stanhope Street* [near Euston, the home of the Terrys]. *Gave Mrs. Terry my large photograph of Tom Taylor, and she gave me photographs of Polly, Florence, Charlie, Tom, and Kate as Ophelia. Before leaving I arranged, as far as it can be done now, to try photographs of the whole party, including Mrs. Watts, in October.*

September was spent at Whitburn photographing, and on returning to town in October Lewis Carroll decided it was too late in the season to start taking the Terrys.

7th APRIL 1865: *Went to Kentish Town, to call on the Terrys. Found the party including Mrs. Watts at home. Their new house has a garden behind, which I hope to use for photography in the summer.*

13th JULY: *Drove over to the Terrys with the camera etc. All are at home except the eldest two boys. It rained a good deal of the day, and I only took three pictures —Polly, Mrs. Watts half-length, and Mrs. Watts with Flo.*

14th JULY: *Spent the day at the Terrys' and took Miss K. Terry, Mr. and Mrs. T., Mrs. Watts* [Plate 47], *a large one of Polly, Polly and Flo* [Plate 46], *Flo, Charlie, etc.*

15th JULY: *Did not get to the Terrys till* 12½, *where I photographed till about* 4½, *taking Kate Terry as "Andromeda"—but draped!—and ending up with "a family group of all but the baby".*

18th JULY: *Took the camera etc. to the Millais, and took a few pictures of the children—all inferior, owing to diffused light* somewhere. *Qu: where?*

19th JULY: *Photographed at Millais' again—still foggy negatives. Can the* [darkroom] *lamp be the cause?*

20th JULY: *To Thomas'—the man there thinks the lamp* is *the cause, as I found when I tried yellow calico round it and got some first-rate negatives, of Mrs. Millais, Effie* [Plate 50] *and Mary* [Plate 51].

21st JULY: *Finished photographing at the Millais' by taking beautiful negatives of Mr. M. and Mary, and a family group* [Plate 49].

25th JULY: *Went down to Windsor with camera etc. and drove over to the Ellises at Cranbourne, where I found they were able to house me, so I got the camera out, and began at once with a good picture of Dymphna* [Plate 52]. On this occasion the photographer did not have with him the album in which he was wont to ask his sitters to sign their names, above which he later pasted their photograph (if it came out!). He had to post it to the Ellises for Dymphna's and her sisters' signatures, and it was duly returned, but not by registered post, which brought forth a gentle reproof in Lewis Carroll's inimitable manner.

Aug. 3rd 1865.

My dear Dymphna,

The photograph-album arrived safe, autographs and all—only the Railway people (who had carefully read it) said that *your* signature made the book "above £10 in value" and that it "ought to have been registered". I told the clerk that was nonsense, and that down at Cranbourne your signature wasn't thought worth 2d., but he shook his head gravely, and said "he knew better than that." . . .

August was again spent at Croft, where—among other children—Aileen Wilson-Todd [Plate 53] and her sisters were photographed.

6th SEPTEMBER: *Left for Ripon on a photographic visit to the Palace.*

7th SEPTEMBER: *Spent most of the day in photographing, and got good pictures of the Bishop* [Bickersteth], *Florence and bird-cage, Ernest, Cyril on wooden horse* [Plate 55], *and a group of Robert and Florence—he in volunteer uniform, as a soldier going off to the wars, and she weeping on his shoulder* ["The Soldier's Farewell"].

8th SEPTEMBER: *Photographing as before—the best I did in the day was a large head of Florence looking out of a window* [Plate 54].

10th APRIL 1866 (London): *To the MacDonalds: they were nearly all at home, and Mr. MacD. walked with me to Dr. Wallich's newly-built house for photography, where we found Dr. and Mrs. Wallich, and a son, Charles. He is quite an enthusiast in the art, which he seems to have adopted as his profession,*[1] *and has built what I should think was the most perfect house for the purpose in London. I suggested that he should undertake printing for amateurs, which is one of the wants of the day, and he seemed to think it worth considering. As Mr. MacD. asked me to go in the evening, when they have some friends, I went back for my large photographs* [to Dowsings Hotel, where Lewis Carroll was staying in London] *and took them first to Dr. Wallich's, where I showed them to him and family. Thence I migrated to the next house, the MacDonalds', where I spent a long evening.*

Impressed by Dr. Wallich's ability, Lewis Carroll went—of his own accord—to his studio to have his portrait taken.

1st MAY (Oxford): *Dined at Prof. Monier Williams'. We had each called on each other twice, but never met before. I thought him pleasant, and Mrs. Williams particularly so. Also I saw the little Ella, whom I had noticed before, and wished to photograph.* He did so on May 24th [Plate 59].

3rd MAY: *Lunched at Prof. Price's to meet Miss Yonge and her mother. It was a pleasure I had long hoped for—and I was very much pleased with her cheerful and easy manners; the sort of person one knows in a few minutes as well as many, in many years. They kindly consented to visit the "studio" to-morrow.*

---

[1] Dr. G. C. Wallich published a series of photographs in book form entitled *Eminent Men of the Day*, 1870.

Charlotte Yonge, the authoress, was one of the three grown-up women whom Lewis Carroll greatly admired. The others were Christina Rossetti [Plate 23] and Ellen Terry [Plate 47]. Whilst he was drawn to the latter by her great charm and brilliant acting, it was chiefly a similarity of outlook on life and religion which attracted him to Charlotte Yonge and Christina Rossetti.

4th MAY: *Mrs. and Miss Yonge came to my rooms at 11, where I showed them a number of photographs, and then to the studio, where I took three tolerably successful pictures of her, one with Mrs. Yonge* [Plate 56] *and two alone* [Plate 57].

On 29th June Lewis Carroll searched for a photographic studio in London. For several years he intended to hire a room to use for one month during the Long Vacation, and to re-let it for the rest of the year. He probably found it irksome to have to bother his friends year after year for permission to turn their house into a studio, and to have to change his *pied-à-terre* several times within a few weeks. Quite understandably he wanted a place of his own (which no doubt would have been a relief to his friends also) where he could photograph to his heart's content, yet he never succeeded in finding one—or a sub-tenant who would agree to his conditions.

8th JULY (Oxford): After enumerating several people whom he has photographed recently—among them Professor and Mrs. Monier Williams—he continues, "*I did several pictures of their little Ella with no other dress than a cloth tied round her, savage-fashion. I also borrowed some New Zealand articles from the Ashmolean, and took a picture of her asleep, covered with a native cloak, and with anklet, etc.*" When grown up, Ella related[1] some of her impressions of Lewis Carroll's photography:

A visit to Mr. Dodgson's rooms to be photographed was always full of surprises. Although he had quaint fancies in the way he dressed his little sitters, he never could bear a dressed-up child.[2] A "natural child" with ruffled untidy hair suited him far better, and he would place her in some ordinary position of daily life, such as sleeping, or reading, and so produce charming pictures.

---

[1] S. D. Collingwood, *The Lewis Carroll Picture Book*, p. 224.

[2] She means in her "Sunday best", for, as we have seen, Lewis Carroll took many costume pictures.

In contradiction to this statement she then immediately relates an attempt at a most *un*natural pose, which the photographer does not elucidate in his diary, though it probably refers to a "ghost" picture (see page 53).

On one occasion he was anxious to obtain a photograph of me as a child sitting up in bed in a fright, with her hair standing on end as if she had seen a ghost. He tried to get this effect with the aid of my father's electrical machine, but it failed, chiefly I fear because I was too young quite to appreciate the current of electricity that had to be passed through me.

24th JULY (London): *After furnishing myself with chemicals at Thomas', I took the camera etc. over to Mr. Sant's* [the artist]. Here Lewis Carroll photographed until 30th July, taking thirty-seven negatives altogether. It was a week of good hunting, and, pleased with the results, the artist enters: "*Never before in one week have I had such lovely children to photograph.*" Following his annual routine, he photographed again in Whitby and at Croft during the Long Vacation.

On 30th November appears a novel reason for a lunch-party. "*Lunched with the Gandells, in order to show Mrs. Gandell how to mount photographs.*"

On 21st May 1867 occurs the first reference to photographing a naked child. "*Mrs. L. brought Beatrice, and I took a photograph of the two; and several of Beatrice alone, 'sans habilement'* " [sic].

30th MAY: *Max Müller* [Professor of Sanskrit, Oxford] *and Mrs. Müller came to be photographed, with the children Ada and Mary (ages about 6 and 5). Quite the loveliest children I have seen for a long while.*

26th JUNE: *Freemasons' fête in the afternoon, where I was introduced to the hero of the day, Mr. Peabody, who kindly consented to sit for a photograph in the morning.* The portrait of the American philanthropist does not seem to have been successful, for album No. III (see page 101) contains his autograph and the date, but no picture.

11th JULY: *Since Commemoration I have been continually photographing and have done some beautiful ones of children—the Owens and the Max Müllers: the former in night-dress, with an actual bed, made several excellent groups.*

Next day Lewis Carroll started on a tour to Russia with Canon Liddon, returning at the end of the Long Vacation. This was the only time he went abroad, and instead of the cumbersome photographic equipment, the sketchbook accompanied him on this trip.

In February 1868 Lewis Carroll wrote a pamphlet in the form of a letter addressed to the Senior Censor of Christ Church. In it he burlesques a paper in which the Department of Experimental Philosophy had detailed the best method of applying certain funds which the Clarendon Trustees had offered to make available. Enumerating the various branches of physics which required additional accommodation, the Department had mentioned photography in their last paragraph:

> As photography is now very much employed in multiplying results of observation, in constructing diagrams for lectures, etc., and as it is in fact a branch of physics, a small photographic room is necessary, both for general use and for studying the subject itself.

In his skit[1] Lewis Carroll enumerates the imaginary requirements of the Mathematical School, and *his* version of the last paragraph reads:

> As photography is now very much employed in recording human expressions, and might possibly be adapted to Algebraical Expressions, a small photographic room would be desirable, both for general use and for representing the various phenomena of Gravity, Disturbance of Equilibrium, Resolution, &c., which affect the features during severe mathematical operations.

Photographic entries begin again in May, but there is nothing worth quoting until

21st JUNE: *My present task is to arrange for the necessary alterations in Lord Bute's rooms, before moving into them, as I have settled to do. There seems a bare possibility of my erecting a photographing room on the top, accessible from the rooms, which would be indeed a luxury, and as I am paying £6 a year rent for my present one* [Badcock's yard], *I should soon save a good deal of the outlay.*

The same day Archdeacon Dodgson died, and Lewis Carroll was too much occupied with family business during the rest of the year to find time for his hobby.

Shortly after their father's death the Misses Dodgson moved to "The Chestnuts", Guildford, Surrey, where in future Lewis Carroll spent nearly every Christmas, and many other vacations. He was there the following Easter, surveying the town for prospective sitters.

23rd AUGUST 1869: *Our first dinner-party in Guildford . . . to the Merrimans, a pleasant family, who will furnish at least one good subject for my camera, Janet, about* 10.

---

[1] Published in *Facts, Figures, and Fancies*, 1874.

On his way from Oxford to Guildford Lewis Carroll had been delayed for three hours in Reading. He went into some public gardens there, where he made the acquaintance of a family named Standen. The day after the short meeting, which led to lifelong friendship, he wrote to Isabel (22nd August), following his usual procedure of introducing himself by sending a copy of *Alice*, but only hinting, for the time being, that C. L. Dodgson and Lewis Carroll might be the same person.

> ... A friend of mine, called Mr. Lewis Carroll, tells me he means to send you a book. He is a *very* dear friend of mine. I have known him all my life (we are the same age) and have *never* left him. Of course he was with me in the gardens, not a yard off—even while I was drawing those puzzles for you. I wonder if you saw him?
>
> Your fifteen-minute friend,
>
> C. L. Dodgson.

A fortnight later he arranged that his new child friend and her sister should be brought over to Guildford to be photographed.

How exceedingly occupied Lewis Carroll was with his hobby on this holiday becomes apparent from the following entries:

3rd SEPTEMBER: *In the last few days I have begun photographing at Guildford.*

17th SEPTEMBER: *I have done little else but photograph.*

5th OCTOBER: *My time has had few events, other than photographic, to mark it, except a week at Torquay with the Argles, which I enjoyed very much. I met their friend Dr. Smith, of whose little girl, Laura, I took some good pictures, including one in a tiger skin ... Most of the time went in photography and walks ... Lately I have taken some capital photographs at Guildford ... Some of the prettiest photographs I have done for some time have been of May and Edith Haydon in their seaside dresses, tunics and knickerbockers—but they do not surpass those I took today of the little Watsons.*

25th JUNE 1870: *Commemoration ... Mr. Synge, from Guildford, was my guest, and I went with him to the Installation of the new Chancellor, Lord Salisbury. I was fortunate enough, by Liddon's intervention, to get the Chancellor's children to photograph—which may be worth detailing. He applied to Lady S. who sent a message through him, consenting, and asking me to go to All Souls' to arrange a time ... The next day Lord S. and party came, and I took negatives of him, alone, and with the two little boys in the dress they wore as his train-bearers.*[1]

6th JULY: *From Ch. Ch. to town with my camera, as the guest of Mr. Holiday.* Henry Holiday was the illustrator of *The Hunting of the Snark* (1876). Using Holiday's house as a base for photography during the next five days, Lewis Carroll took pictures of a large number of children, including many he had photographed on previous visits to London, and concluded the series with a group of his host with his wife and daughter. From the Holidays he went to the MacDonalds' new home at Hammersmith, where two more days were spent photographing. Some years later, perhaps infected by Lewis Carroll's enthusiasm for the art, Henry Holiday also took up photography, and became a member of the Photographic Society of London in May 1891.

25th APRIL 1871: *On Sunday I added to my list of friends in Oxford by joining Arnold (of University College) in the Parks, where he was walking with his children, and going back with him to his house. Of course I arranged to photograph the children, Julia (8) and Ethel (6).*

5th JUNE: *I went off, soon after 11, to borrow Julia Arnold for a photograph. Brought her back (with Ethel) and did a very good negative of her in Chinese dress (I had to do it now, in order to return the dress to Mrs. Foster, who lent it me).*

14th JUNE: *Commemoration, which I did* not *attend, and Freemasons' fête, which I did attend, and where I found two new subjects for the camera, children of Capt. Fane.*

15th JUNE: *I called on Mrs. Fane, to make acquaintance and thank them for consenting to my proposal, and was much pleased with the two girls, Agnes and Isabel.*

In July Lewis Carroll stayed for a few days with Lord Salisbury at Hatfield House, the magnificent seat of the Cecil family, in Hertfordshire, and borrowed camera and chemicals from the chaplain in order to take a photograph of the children.

---

[1] Album No. III contains only the autographs of Lord Salisbury and his sons. The photograph is reproduced in S. D. Collingwood's *Life and Letters of Lewis Carroll,* p. 141.

17th MARCH 1872: *Yesterday I took my first photo in the new studio—Julia Arnold.* The glass-house had been ready since the previous October, but apparently the photographer was too much occupied with other work to make use of it.

31st MAY: *Took three boxes of negatives to Hills & Saunders, including a view of the new wooden belfry[1] taken from the roof.* Though only a temporary erection, the simple wooden structure caused Lewis Carroll much annoyance, and he attacked it in several sarcastic pamphlets, notably *The New Belfry of Christ Church.*

18th JUNE: *A most successful day. Mrs. Simpson, Gaynor and Amy, came over by the 6 a.m. train, stayed till 5.35. I gave them breakfast and dinner, took six good photographs of the children, and shewed them S. John's, Worcester, etc.* This occasion marks the beginning of Lewis Carroll's correspondence with Gaynor Simpson, who in one of her letters asked whether he were fond of dancing, not aware that he had already mathematically defined its value to him some years previously:[2]

Yet what are all such gaieties to me
Whose thoughts are full of indices and surds?

$$x^2 + 7x + 53$$
$$= \tfrac{11}{3}$$

Gaynor made a bad start by addressing him as "Mr. Dodson" (as the name is in fact pronounced), which elicited an inimitable reply in the typical Carrollian vein.

My dear Gaynor,   *December 27 1873.*

My name is spelt with a "G", that is to say "*Dodgson*". Any one who spells it the same as that wretch (I mean of course the Chairman of Committees in the House of Commons) offends me *deeply*, and *for ever*! It is a thing I *can* forget, but *never can forgive*! If you do it again, I shall call you "'Aynor". Could you live happy with such a name?
As to dancing, my dear, I *never* dance, unless I am allowed to do it *in my own peculiar way*. There is no use trying to describe it: it has to be seen to be believed. The last house I tried it in, the floor broke through. But then it

---

[1] This photograph is contained in album No. III.
[2] "Four Riddles", *Phantasmagoria*, 1869.

69

was a poor sort of floor—the beams were only six inches thick, hardly worth calling beams at all: stone arches are much more sensible, when any dancing, *of my peculiar kind*, is to be done. Did you ever see the Rhinoceros, and the Hippopotamus, at the Zoological Gardens, trying to dance a minuet together? It is a touching sight . . .

There are no more entries in 1872 after 25th July, but the first entry in 1873, on 30th January, is interesting, for it proves that the new studio made the photographer independent of weather and season. *"Took a photograph (remarkably good for the winter) of Helen Feilden"*; on 7th May he notes, *"I did two photos in heavy rain."*
This year is full of short memoranda of interest only to the photographer himself. We would merely mention in passing that from now on Lewis Carroll indulged ever increasingly in costume pictures, dressing up his child friends as Roman girls, in Greek dress, in Indian shawls, in Danish costume, as Chinamen, in South Sea Island costume, in beach dress, and occasionally still further undressing until there was no costume at all. The chief sitters during this period were Julia and Ethel Arnold, Alexandra (Xie) Kitchin—who was posed one afternoon in three different fancy pictures, *"with spade and bucket, in bed, and in Greek dress"*—and the two elder daughters of the Rev. Edwin Hatch, Beatrice and Ethel. It was in this year also that Lewis Carroll began making *carte-de-visite* and cabinet-size photographs.

15th JANUARY 1874: *I called on the Holidays and found him, Mrs. H. and Winnie. He showed me the drawings he is doing for me (suggestions for groups of two children—nude studies—for me to try to reproduce in photographs from life), which are quite exquisite.* Back in Oxford Lewis Carroll at once set to work. He wrote to Mrs. Hatch, "As I shall be here for two or three days more and the mornings are lovely for photography, couldn't you come over to-morrow or next day, any time between 10 and 1, and bring Birdie, or better, Birdie and Ethel? You shall see the drawings Wm. [sic] Holiday made as guides for me, and then you can have the bairns photographed in that or any other dress you may prefer."

23rd MARCH: *Took a photograph of Mowbray, M.P. for Oxford Univ., and three of Xie Kitchin (for first time this year).*
In the middle of May, Henry Holiday stayed with Lewis Carroll for a few days.

18th MAY: *He fetched Xie Kitchin to be photographed, and I did a large one, full length, lying on the sofa in a long night-gown, which H. arranged—about the best I have ever done of her.* Soon afterwards Lewis Carroll met Xie's father and asked him if he knew how to get excellence from a photo. The Rev. G. W. Kitchin was at a loss for an answer. "All you have got to do is to get a lens and put Xie before it." (Note: "Xie" is pronounced "Ecksy.")[1]

Henry Holiday's visit, and his own photographic studies from life, seem to have re-awakened Lewis Carroll's interest in figure drawing, for he writes

27th JUNE: *I have begun again drawing from life.* These sketches from life, in which he painstakingly tried to copy nature, are worthless and stand in complete contrast to the brilliant pen illustrations with which he so often embellished his early writings. Whenever he drew upon his immensely fertile imagination, as in the illustrations to *Misch-Masch*, *The Rectory Umbrella* and the MS. of *Alice's Adventures Under Ground*, Lewis Carroll revealed a talent by far surpassing that of his illustrators, with the possible exception of Sir John Tenniel. The caricatures of the "Pictures in the Vernon Gallery" and "Studies from English Poets" have the same masterly touch as his literary burlesques, and we are the poorer for the circumstance that Lewis Carroll was dissuaded from cultivating this talent by John Ruskin, "who was always willing to assist him with his valuable advice on any point of artistic criticism" and who "told him that he had not enough talent to make it worth his while to devote much time to sketching".[2] Naturally, to a critic to whom the highest criterion in art was anatomical correctness and truth to nature, Lewis Carroll's grotesque illustrations were anathema. Was it due to Ruskin's influence that Lewis Carroll abandoned the idea of publishing his own illustrations to *Alice*—"designs that rebelled against every law of Anatomy or Art (for I had never had a lesson in drawing)"?[3] Lewis Carroll's apology would point in that direction, and trusting implicitly in the guidance of the Apostle of Pre-Raphaelitism, he quite

---

[1] This excruciating pun was related many years later in a letter from Brook Kitchin to Beatrice Hatch.

[2] S. D. Collingwood, *Life and Letters of Lewis Carroll*, 1898.

[3] Lewis Carroll, "Alice on the Stage", *The Theatre*, April 1887.

understandably also used this strait-jacket on his artist collaborators, exhorting them to concentrate on drawing from life, or from photographs which he liberally supplied.

Harry Furniss, illustrator of the two *Sylvie and Bruno* books (and also, later on, Miss Gertrude Thomson), used to receive batches of photographs when he corresponded with Lewis Carroll about the heroine's appearance. In his outspoken account[1] he tells of "reams of written descriptions and piles of useless photographs intended to inspire me to draw with a few lines a face embodying his ideal in a space not larger than a threepenny piece. By one post I would receive a batch of photographs of some young lady Lewis Carroll fancied had one feature, or half a feature, of that ideal he had conjured up in his mind as his heroine." Furniss was expected to collect fragments of faces, from Land's End to John o' Groats: to see a perfect nose in Glasgow, to study the eyes of a girl living at Eastbourne, and the ears of a vicar's daughter in Brighton.

Since Ruskin's day, canons of art have undergone many changes to suit new environments and periods. Our outlook has perceptibly widened; we have set ourselves higher ideals than mere verisimilitude, and having gradually become accustomed, to a lesser or greater degree, to all sorts of abstractions and distortions in modern art, we bring a better understanding to Lewis Carroll's sketches than did his contemporaries. Yet how complex is the question of aesthetic appreciation! The same men and women who would have been shocked by Lewis Carroll's imaginative illustrations enthusiastically accepted his "surrealist" stories and nonsense verses, which one might have expected to have been equally unpalatable to Victorian taste.

3rd JULY (Oxford): *I think of staying a week or so to finish up stray bits of business and collect what I want to take with me for the "Long". I hope to pay photographic visits to [Henry] Holiday and Moray Lodge*[2] *and to do a good spell of work in the Isle of Wight (perhaps at Sandown), including my Euclid I and II and book on "Elections". I think of taking my camera too, and trying some child subjects (in which the island abounds).* In September he did go to Sandown, where he found plenty of new photographic subjects.

---

[1] Harry Furniss, *The Confessions of a Caricaturist*, 1901.

[2] Moray Lodge, Camden Hill, London, the home of Mrs. Arthur Lewis (Kate Terry).

In 1875 Lewis Carroll's photographic activity began on 15th May. Two days later a Mrs. Harcourt came with one of her sisters to have a lesson in photography.

24th MAY: *Mr. Vaughan, foreman at Parkers, came to show me the process of taking photos (Wortley's) without a bath.*[1] *It does not seem to give such good definition as the ordinary process.* Afterwards Lewis Carroll dined with the Harcourts and gave Mrs. Harcourt more advice about fitting up her darkroom. We also learn that he wrote to R. H. Collins, tutor to Prince Leopold (Queen Victoria's youngest son), then an undergraduate at Christ Church, to ask if the Prince would sit for a photo. The following day came a note giving the Prince's consent, with an invitation to lunch—a friendly gesture that must have gratified Lewis Carroll's long-standing desire for intercourse with royalty.

26th MAY: *Paid my first (possibly my only) visit to Wykeham House. We were six at luncheon, there being a Dr. Hoffman (or some such name—a physician in attendance, I believe) and two junior men. I found myself treated as senior guest, and had to sit next to the young host, who was particularly unassuming and genial in manner: I do not wonder at his being so universal a favourite. After lunch we adjourned to a large tent in the garden, where coffee and cigars were provided. I showed the Prince a few photographs I had taken with me, and after arranging for a sitting on Wednesday next, took my leave.*

2nd JUNE: *The Prince came alone about 11½, and was joined afterwards by Collins. He staid [sic] till nearly 1, and I took two photographs of him* [Plate 63], *but neither was quite free from moving. He looked over a number of photographs, and chose some for me to give him.*

3rd JUNE: *With some difficulty I persuaded Ruskin to come and be photographed, and to stay luncheon with us.* (Two of Lewis Carroll's sisters were on a visit to Oxford.)

9th JUNE: *Went over to Tunbridge Wells to leave the negatives of Prince Leopold, and others, with Robinson and Cherrill.*

In July, when in London, Lewis Carroll called on Mr. Heatherley,

---

[1] In 1873 Col. Stuart Wortley had started the commercial manufacture of dry collodion plates, which contained, in addition to rubber (the preservative substance), a yellowish-red dye to prevent halation, a defect from which collodion plates had suffered to some extent in the past. With such ready-prepared plates the silver nitrate sensitising bath was dispensed with.

owner of a well-known art school, and borrowed some Chinese and other dresses, including a suit of chain armour, and the next week was spent in photographing a number of acquaintances in these costumes.

12th JULY: *A grand day of photos. Did the du Maurier children, and the Terrys; Polly in armour, and as "Dora"; and Florence as a Turk.*

31st JULY (Oxford): *The week has gone in registering and arranging photos—at about 10 h. work per day.*

7th/8th AUGUST: *Another week has gone exactly like the last—in photographic registering etc. I have now got the alphabetical index of negatives arranged and nearly complete—written up the chronological register nearly to date—numbered, by it, all unmounted prints and mounted cartes and cabinets, and arranged them—numbered nearly all mounted in albums, and entered in the register references to them—and gone through all the $4\frac{1}{4} \times 3\frac{1}{4}$ and 6×5 negatives by means of the register, erasing some, finding places for others, and making out an order for new prints to be done by Hills and Saunders. I find I must adopt some other plan to keep the negatives from* damp—*shut-up boxes have ruined many of my best. I think of having all the lids removed, and the sides of the boxes, and the panels of the cupboard, pierced with holes. The remaining photo business is to go through the $7\frac{1}{4} \times 6\frac{1}{4}$, $8\frac{1}{2} \times 6\frac{1}{2}$ and 10×8 negatives—to select some more cabinets for "show" bundles, and a bundle of "show" cartes—to mount on larger cards some of the new prints, also for show. The mounting prints in albums I leave for the winter. I hope to get all done this week. I dined with Harvey and his wife last Sunday; and Harcourt and his wife dined with me on Monday—otherwise I have led the life of a hermit.*

11th/12th AUGUST: *I have now gone through all the negatives, and copied into a little book the order for prints—the largest I have ever given. Several of the negative boxes have now been turned into upright crates, and seem to answer very well.*

24th OCTOBER: *A sudden idea occurred, about which I wrote to Holiday and Macmillan, of publishing the "Snark" poem this Christmas—also of writing an acrostic on "Gertrude Chataway"* [whom he had met that summer at Sandown] *which I did the same night.*

25th OCTOBER: *Finished the verses and sent them to Mrs. Chataway, asking leave to print them. I think they might do for a dedication to the book, which I think of calling "The Hunting of the Snark". It also occurs to me that such a publication would give me a good opportunity of circulating two papers (which*

74

might be lightly gummed in)—one a new "Christmas Greeting" to my 40,000
*child-readers—the other an advertisement for a house (and garden perhaps) in or
near London, where I might put up a studio, and take portraits for about a month
each summer. It might be used at other times by some other photographer.*[1] The
priceless idea of circulating a personal advertisement in a book—and
in incongruous combination with a Christmas greeting—was dropped.
It would certainly have been unique in book publication, but no doubt
Macmillan's refused to countenance it. Instead, Lewis Carroll soon hit
upon another novel idea which he seems to have carried out. On 7th
November he wrote to Mrs. Chataway, whom he had already asked
for some photographs of Gertrude in beach dress, "When I receive the
two cartes of Gertrude in beach attire, may I order a few unmounted
prints of the best from Debenham? I want to insert them in a few
copies of the book, opposite the dedicatory verses—if you remember
which it was I admired most perhaps you would order half-a-dozen
unmounted prints, which would save time." *The Hunting of the Snark*
was published at Easter 1876 and the dedicatory verses referred to
contain a double acrostic on the name of the girl, who was Lewis Carroll's leading child friend during the next ten years. He wrote her the
most lovely nonsense conceivable and Gertrude naturally revelled in it.

My dear Gertrude,   *Dec. 9 1875.*

This really will *not* do, you know, sending one more kiss every time by
post: the parcel gets so heavy it is quite expensive. When the postman
brought in the last letter, he looked quite grave. "Two pounds to pay, sir!"
he said. "*Extra weight*, sir!" (I think he cheats a little, by the way. He
often makes me pay two *pounds*, when I think it should be *pence*.) "Oh, if
you please, Mr. Postman!" I said, going down gracefully on one knee
(I wish you could see me go down on one knee to a postman—it's a very
pretty sight), "do excuse me just this once! It's only from a little girl!"
"Only from a little girl!" he growled. "What are little girls made of?"
"Sugar and spice", I began to say, "and all that's ni—" but he interrupted
me. "No! I don't mean *that*. I mean, what's the good of little girls, when
they send such heavy letters?" "Well, they're not *much* good, certainly",
I said, rather sadly.
"Mind you don't get any more such letters", he said, "at least, not from
that particular little girl. *I know her well, and she's a regular bad one.*" That's
not true, is it? I don't believe he ever saw you, and you're not a bad one,

---

[1] See also p. 64, entry for 29th June 1866.

are you? However, I promised him we would send each other very few more letters—"Only two thousand four hundred and seventy, or so," I said. "Oh!" he said, "a little number like *that* doesn't signify. What I meant is, you mustn't send *many*."

So you see we must keep count now, and when we get to two thousand four hundred and seventy, we mustn't write any more, unless the postman gives us leave.

I sometimes wish I was back on the shore at Sandown; don't you?

Your loving friend,

Lewis Carroll.

In 1876, the entries relating to photography begin again in May.

15th JULY: *Spent 4 hours over family album, in making up index, selecting new photographs etc. and mounted a few of the new ones* and with that pedantic delight with which he calculated everything, even the time it would take were he to accept a million hugs and kisses which a little girl sent him in a letter, he reckoned that *"mounting photos (including finding and cutting out the print) takes about 9 m. apiece."*

18th OCTOBER (Oxford): *Having no lectures, I got Mrs. —— to bring Lily at 11; but all photographs failed, owing to the developer being made (apparently) of bad protosulphate of iron. Got Mr. Forshaw (the operator at Hills & Saunders) to come over, and with his developer we got very good results.*

20th OCTOBER: *A very dull afternoon, yet I got two good negatives of Lily— one seated on a low chair, and one standing with wand . . . It is quite a new privilege to have a subject for photography so entirely indifferent as to dress: I have had none such since B.H., July* 30/73.

23rd OCTOBER: *Mounted two prints of "Lily with wand"; it is the quickest piece of photography I have done, as the negative was only done three days ago.*

26th OCTOBER: *Began photographing soon after breakfast, and did the last (eleven in the day) about ½ past 3. I took eight of Gertrude* [Chataway], *one each of Mrs. and Miss C. and one of May Barker.*

28th OCTOBER: *In spite of the dull morning I did three very successful pictures (smaller lens—large diaphragm—45 seconds each).*

13th JANUARY 1877: *Went up to town for the day, and took Evelyn with me to the afternoon pantomime at the Adelphi—"Goody Two-Shoes", acted entirely by children. It was a really charming performance. Little Bertie Coote, aged ten, was clown—a wonderfully clever little fellow; and Carrie Coote, about eight, was*

Columbine, a very pretty graceful little thing. In a few years' time she will be just the *child to act "Alice", if it is ever dramatised. The Harlequin was a little girl named Gilchrist[1], one of the most beautiful children, in face and figure, that I have ever seen. I must get an opportunity of photographing her.*

10th APRIL: *Spent the day in London. Called on Mrs. Gilchrist and spent about half an hour with her and Connie. I was decidedly pleased with Connie, who has a refined and modest manner, with just a touch of shyness, and who is about the most gloriously beautiful child (both face and figure) that I ever saw. One would like to do 100 photographs of her.*

15th APRIL: *Devised a plan for getting photos of C. Gilchrist: to be staying in London; to bring her over to Oxford by the early train, and take her back in the evening; this would give nine hours in Oxford and cost little more than paying for her and an escort, who would be an encumbrance.*

15th JUNE: *Had studio etc. dusted* [this seems to be an event rare enough to be worthy of record; the last entry to this effect was on 19th October 1876] *and mixed some chemicals, as I hope to do a few photographs here this month. All seems to be in good working order.*

16th JUNE: *Mrs. Hatch brought Beatrice and Ethel, and I photo'd both, the latter in Turkish dress.* These were the first photographs in 1877. In 1878, entries begin again in May.

26th JUNE (in London for the day): *Arranged with Mrs. Coote to sell me three old theatrical dresses of Carrie's* [see entry of 13th January 1877, opposite], *besides the new Prince's dress, which she is making for me.*

I will now give a few entries from a typical page in the diary, just to show that although my quotations have become fewer, because the entries are too trivial in content to merit the permanence of print, they have by no means ceased. Lewis Carroll went on photographing with undiminished zeal: whoever called on him was at once placed before the lens.

23rd OCTOBER: *Mrs. Feilden and Helen called, and I took two photos of the latter.*

26th OCTOBER: *Mrs. Woodroffe and Clara spent the day with me. I photographed both.*

---

[1] Connie Gilchrist later achieved fame at the Gaiety, married the seventh Earl of Orkney in 1892, and died in 1946 at the age of eighty-one.

1st NOVEMBER: *Henderson brought his two little girls, Annie and Frances: I took a photo of Annie.*

12th NOVEMBER: *Mr. F. A. Smith* [a rector at Shrewsbury] *called and I took a photograph of him.*

20th NOVEMBER: *Barclay Thompson brought Mrs. B.T. to see me, and I took a photo of her.*

22nd NOVEMBER: *Pember called, and I took a photo of him.*

Again there are few outstanding events the following year. Mr. Bowles, Editor of *Vanity Fair*, came to be photographed in March. In June, Lewis Carroll was at Guildford and spent several hours at the house of a clergyman friend *"giving photographic hints to his pupil"*.

27th JUNE 1879 (London): *To the S. Kensington Museum, to meet (by appointment) Miss E. G. Thomson, who is staying in town, and whom I had not met before. She had her sketch-book with her, and showed me some lovely bits she had done from antiques.*

The meeting with Miss Thomson, the last of Lewis Carroll's collaborators, was described at greater length by the artist herself,[1] and though it is, strictly speaking, outside the scope of this book, I think it is worth quoting here all the same, since it enlarges our picture of Lewis Carroll.

A little before twelve I was at the rendezvous, and then the humour of the situation suddenly struck me, that *I* had not the ghost of an idea what *he* was like, nor would *he* have any better chance of discovering *me*! . . . At that moment a gentleman entered, two little girls clinging to his hands, and as I caught sight of the tall slim figure, with the clean-shaven, delicate, refined face, I said to myself, *"That's* Lewis Carroll." He stood for a moment, head erect, glancing swiftly over the room, then, bending down, whispered something to one of the children; she, after a moment's pause, pointed straight at me.

Dropping their hands he came forward, and with that winning smile of his that utterly banished the oppressive sense of the Oxford don, said simply, "I am Mr. Dodgson; I was to meet you, I think?" To which I as frankly smiled, and said, "How did you know me so soon?"

"My little friend found you. I told her I had come to meet a young lady who knew fairies, and she fixed on you at once. But *I* knew you before she spoke."

4th JULY: *Called, by appointment, on Sir F.* [Frederick] *Leighton, whom I*

---

[1] Article in *The Gentlewoman*, 29th January 1898.

had never seen before and whom I was much taken with. He showed me some lovely unfinished paintings . . . a standing figure in green drapery, with a child leaning over and kissing her . . . (He recommends the child for Miss Thomson, who wants a model.)

A fortnight later Miss Thomson came to Oxford, bringing Sir Frederick Leighton's little model with her. *"I did an ordinary portrait of her, and six* [nude] *'studies', in arranging which Miss Thomson was of great use."*

18th JULY: [An Oxford mother brought her two little girls to the studio.] *I had warned Mrs. —— that I thought the children so nervous I would not even ask for "bare feet" and was agreeably surprised to find they were ready for any amount of undress, and seemed delighted at being allowed to run about naked. It was a great privilege to have such a model as —— to take: a* very *pretty face, and a good figure. She was worth any number of my model of yesterday.*

During this month there are many references to Oxford children being photographed in the artist's favourite dress of "nothing", lying on a blanket, or on the sofa—*"a kind of photograph I have often done lately"*.

24th MAY 1880: *Percival, President of Trinity College, who has Cardinal Newman as his guest, wrote to say that the cardinal would sit for a photo to me, at Trinity. But I could not take my photography there, and he couldn't come to me: so nothing came of it.*

31st MAY: *Abp. Tait* [of York] *(who is visiting at Balliol) came at my request to be photographed. He brought with him his two daughters—very pleasant girls.* Archbishop Tait had been Lewis Carroll's headmaster at Rugby.

18th JUNE: *A sunny morning, which I gave to printing, and by 1 had got twenty-three prints ready for toning. Then I went and fetched Annie and Frances Henderson, and did five good negatives. After taking them back, I went to work at toning and fixing, and just got all finished by 7.*

30th JUNE: *Sorting and erasing negatives—the number on hand is far too great.*

15th JULY: *Spent morning in printing. Gertrude and Gerida Drage came at 3, and I spent two hours in photographing them: then toning, fixing etc. till 7.*

This is the last entry relating to Lewis Carroll's photography. There is no indication why he suddenly gave up his hobby, but I have no doubt that the reason was not of a technical nature, as has been suggested by more than one writer. Their assumption is based chiefly on the fact that Lewis Carroll disliked the dry-plate process which in that year almost completely superseded the collodion wet plate. It does not seem to have occurred to them that there was nothing to prevent him from continuing to prepare his plates by the old method, which is in fact still employed by many process-engravers.

The artistic inferiority of dry-plate photography complained of by Lewis Carroll in a letter to Gertrude Thomson (see below) was, of course, due to the vast increase in the number of amateurs who swelled the ranks of photographers, attracted by the much simplified and cleaner darkroom manipulation which was one of the great advantages of manufactured plates and roll-films. The other advantage was their increased sensitivity, which opened up the way to instantaneous photography and brought in its wake a great number of hand cameras which made snapshooting a pastime for many enthusiasts who were entirely devoid of artistic training and feeling, and—like the great majority of present-day amateurs—aimlessly frittered away their roll-films for the simple reason that in their hands the camera had degenerated into a toy and ceased to be a means of expression. In the mid-eighties, and in particular in 1888 with the introduction of the "Kodak", with which 100 exposures could be taken consecutively, photography underwent a revolution comparable only with that which the introduction of the collodion process wrought in the early eighteen-fifties.

In the letter to Miss Thomson, which is dated 9th July 1893— exactly thirteen years after he had given up photography—Lewis Carroll says:

All "dry plate" photography is inferior, in artistic effect, to the now abandoned "wet plate", but as a means of making *memoranda* of attitudes etc. it is invaluable. Every figure artist ought to practise it. If I had a dry-plate camera, and time to work it, and could secure a child of really good figure, either a professional model, or (much better) a child of the upper classes, I would put her into every pretty attitude I could think of, and could get in a single morning 50 or 100 such memoranda. Do try this with the next pretty child you get as a model and let me have some of the photos.

Since Miss Thomson belonged to that class of "artists" who need photographs to assist them in their drawings, it was natural for her to submit her photographs to Lewis Carroll's criticism, just as he submitted his sketches to her; and if he found fault with her pictures, would he not, in his polite and indirect way of putting things, blame any shortcomings on the process rather than on the artist?

Feeling certain that the letter does not indicate Lewis Carroll's reason for giving up his hobby, I have come to the conclusion that his decision was not connected with photography at all.

Lewis Carroll suffered from a morbid fear that he might not live to finish the many literary projects which he had on hand, and in order to devote his time entirely to writing—the one thing he felt mattered most—he changed his whole mode of life. He resigned the mathematical lectureship on 18th October 1881 (when only forty-nine years old) for the following reasons: "*I shall now have my whole time at my disposal, and, if God gives me life and continued health and strength, may hope, before my powers fail, to do some worthy work in writing—partly in the cause of mathematical education, partly in the cause of innocent recreation for children, and partly, I hope (though so utterly unworthy of being allowed to take up such work) in the cause of religious thought. May God bless the new form of life that lies before me, that I may use it according to His holy will.*"

To this end he had sacrificed first his hobby, then his lectureship, and now he decided to refuse social invitations.

5th MAY 1884: *Wrote to* ——, *who had invited me to dine, to beg off, on the ground that, in my old age* [fifty-two!] *I find dinner parties more and more fatiguing. It is quite a new departure. I much grudge giving an evening (even if it were not tiring) to bandying small-talk with dull people.*"

About this time Lewis Carroll used to spend a good twelve hours a day in reading and writing, and on 29th March 1885 he entered: "*Never before have I had so many literary projects on hand at once*", listing fifteen intended publications or new editions.

The fear of not being able to finish his work preyed incessantly on his mind. Is it not somewhat premature for a man in excellent health to write at the age of fifty-eight: "*As life shortens in and the evening shadows loom in sight, one gets to* grudge any *time given to mere pleasure, which might entail the leaving work half finished that one is longing to do before the end comes . . . There is one text that often occurs to me, 'The night cometh, when no man can work.'* "

He never grudged the time spent with children, though his sense of class distinction, so openly manifested in his letter to Beatrice Hatch, seems to have become more acute in later years. Beatrice Hatch was one of the few girls whose friendship with Lewis Carroll endured beyond childhood. She did social work in Oxford, and in the first part of this letter (which is dated 16th February 1894) Lewis Carroll congratulates her on having so orderly a set of girls to deal with, and says that it was a real pleasure to see so many bright and happy faces.

Though he had given up his only hobby, the company of little girls still warmed his heart. They were invited—one at a time—to accompany him on a walk, or to have tea in his rooms, and as a special treat might be taken to one of the London theatres or even privileged to stay with him for a few weeks at Oxford or Eastbourne. For their portrait, he now took his little friends to professional photographers such as Henry Herschel Hay Cameron in London, W. Kent in Eastbourne (where he spent the last seventeen summer holidays), and others.

It is amusing to see how every event leads Lewis Carroll's thoughts back to his former hobby. In recording the death of the Rev. E. Hatch, for instance, in November 1889, he notes: "*A friend of many years standing, whose daughter Beatrice, now grown up, was as a baby-child a favourite photo subject of mine.*" Is this not somewhat reminiscent of Mrs. Cameron's inconsequential—or is it consequential?—remark in her *Annals of My Glass House*? *A propos* the marriage of her former maid and model she comments, "and what is of far more importance, [it is] a marriage of bliss with children worthy of being *photographed*, as their mother had been, for their beauty".

PLATES

1.   LEWIS CARROLL. Portrait by O. G. Rejlander

2. MR. BENN, a friend of the Dodgson family

3. THREE GIRLS. Taken at Croft Rectory

4. "COATES", daughter of an employee at Croft Rectory

5.   ALICE MURDOCH. One of Lewis Carroll's earliest portraits

6. SIX OF LEWIS CARROLL'S SISTERS AND HIS BROTHER EDWIN

7. LOUISA, MARGARET AND HENRIETTA DODGSON

8. ALFRED, LORD TENNYSON, Poet Laureate

9. HALLAM TENNYSON, son of the Poet Laureate

10. AGNES GRACE WELD as "Little Red Riding-Hood"

II. THE MISSES LUTWIDGE, two of Lewis Carroll's aunts

of her own little sister. So the boat wound slowly along, beneath the bright summer-day, with its merry crew and its music of voices and laughter, till. it passed round one of the many turnings of the stream, and she saw it no more.

Then she thought, (in a dream within the dream, as it were,) how this same little Alice would, in the after-time., be herself a grown woman: and how she would keep, through her riper years, the simple and loving heart of her childhood; and how she would gather around her other little children, and make _their_ eyes bright and eager with many a wonderful tale, perhaps even with these very adventures of the little Alice of long-ago: and how she would feel with all their simple sorrows, and find a pleasure in all their simple joys, remembering her own child-life, and the happy summer days.

12. LAST PAGE OF MS. *Alice's Adventures Under Ground* with portrait of ALICE LIDDELL

13. AGNES GRACE WELD, Mrs. Tennyson's niece

Beatrice Henley.

14. BEATRICE HENLEY, daughter of the Vicar at Putney

15. ALICE JANE DONKIN posing for "The Elopement"

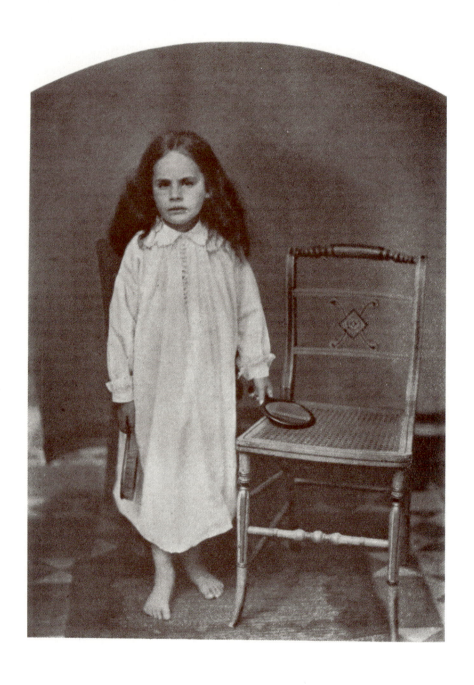

16.   IRENE MACDONALD.   "It Won't Come Smooth"

IRENE MAC DONAED

17. IRENE MACDONALD, daughter of George Macdonald

18. WICLIFFE TAYLOR, son of Tom Taylor

19. TOM TAYLOR, Editor of *Punch*

20. MARCUS KEANE

D. Gabriel Rossetti

Oct 6 1863

21.   DANTE GABRIEL ROSSETTI, poet and painter

22. ALPHONSE LEGROS, Slade Professor at London University

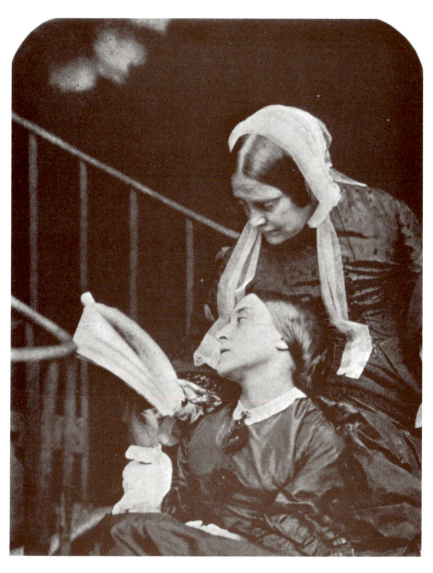

Christina G. Rossetti   *Frances Rossetti*

23. CHRISTINA ROSSETTI and her mother

24. MRS. ROSSETTI WITH DANTE GABRIEL, CHRISTINA, AND WILLIAM MICHAEL

25. ALEXANDER MUNRO, THE SCULPTOR, WITH HIS WIFE

Zoe Strong

26. ZOE STRONG, a relative of Dr. T. B. Strong, Dean of Christ Church

27.   HELENE BEYER, a German model employed by Dante Gabriel Rossetti

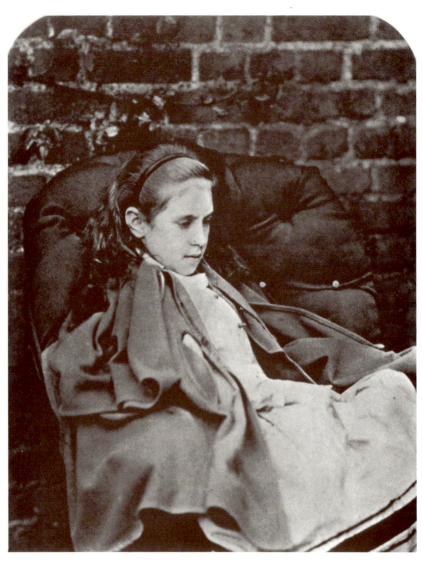

Mary Josephine MacDonald

28. MARY MACDONALD, daughter of George Macdonald

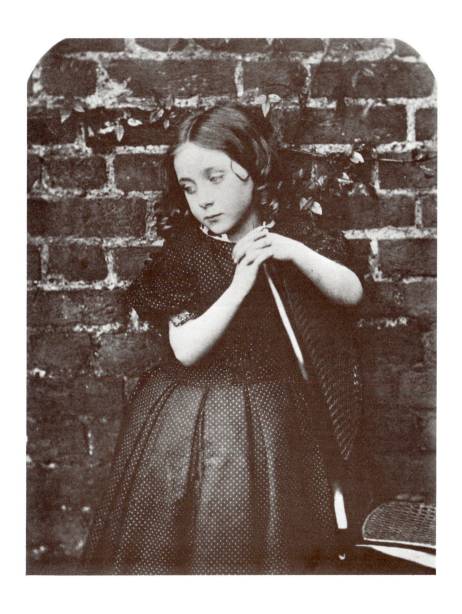

29. AMY HUGHES, daughter of Arthur Hughes, the artist

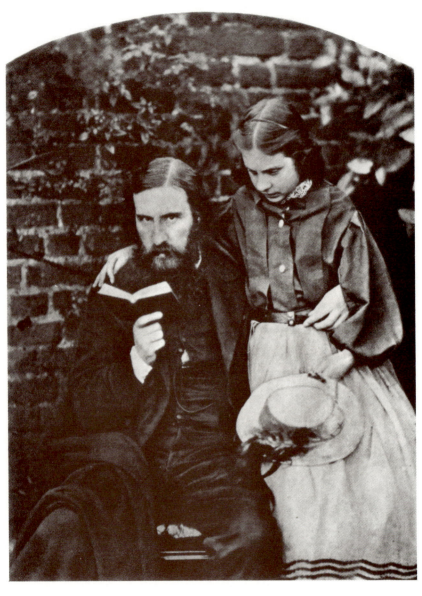

George MacDonald *Lily Scott MacDonald*

30. GEORGE MACDONALD, NOVELIST AND POET, WITH HIS ELDEST DAUGHTER, LI

Greville M. MacDonald

31. GREVILLE MACDONALD, son of George Macdonald

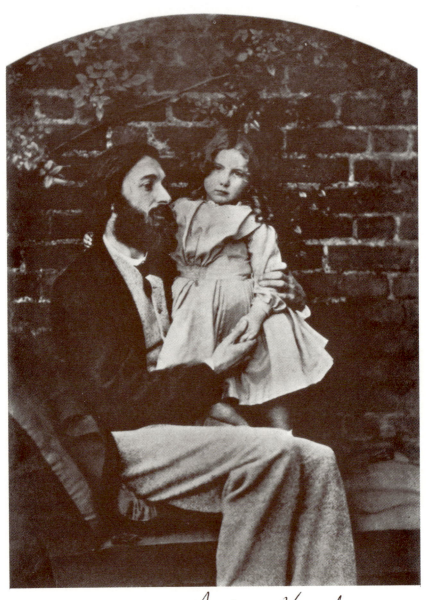

Arthur Hughes

Oct 12 .63

32.   ARTHUR HUGHES, THE ARTIST, AND HIS DAUGHTER AGNES

Arthur Hughes.

33.   ARTHUR HUGHES, JR.

Agnes Florence Price

34. AGNES FLORENCE PRICE, daughter of Professor Bartholomew Price

Frederick Crown Prince of Denmark
November 18th 1863.

35.   FREDERICK, Crown Prince of Denmark

36.   ELIZABETH HUSSEY, daughter of Professor Robert Hussey

37.   REV. C. BARKER AND HIS DAUGHTER MAY

38.   IVO BLIGH, son of Lord Darnley

39.   GRACE DENMAN, daughter of Lord Chief Justice Denman

Madeline Catherine Parnell

40. MADELINE CATHERINE PARNELL, niece of Mrs. Longley

41. DR. C. T. LONGLEY, Archbishop of Canterbury

Alice Constance

42. ALICE CONSTANCE WESTMACOTT, daughter of the sculptor Richard Westmacott

43. MARIA WHITE, niece of the porter at Lambeth Palace

44. MRS. FRANKLIN AND HER DAUGHTER ROSE

45. ALICE LIDDELL

Polly Terry

46. MARION AND FLORENCE, sisters of Ellen Terry

Truly yours
Ellen Alice Watts:

47. ELLEN TERRY at the age of eighteen

John Everett Millais

48.   JOHN EVERETT MILLAIS, Pre-Raphaelite painter

Effie C. Millais

49. MR. AND MRS. MILLAIS WITH THEIR TWO DAUGHTERS

Effie Millais

50. **EFFIE MILLAIS,** daughter of John Millais

Mary Millais

51. MARY MILLAIS, daughter of John Millais

Dymphna Ellis.

52. DYMPHNA ELLIS, daughter of the Rector of Cranbourne

Aileen

53. AILEEN WILSON-TODD, taken at Croft Rectory

Florence Bickersteth.

54. FLORENCE BICKERSTETH, daughter of the Bishop of Ripon

Cyril Bickersteth

55. CYRIL BICKERSTETH, son of the Bishop of Ripon

56. MRS. YONGE AND HER DAUGHTER CHARLOTTE

57. CHARLOTTE M. YONGE, the famous novelist

58.   ALICE EMILY DONKIN AND HER COUSIN ALICE JANE DONKIN

Ella Chlora Williams

59. ELLA MONIER-WILLIAMS, daughter of Professor Monier-Williams

Katie Brine.

60. KATIE BRINE, granddaughter of Dr. Pusey

John Phillips
July 11 1866

61. PROFESSOR JOHN PHILLIPS, F.R.S., the geologist

ALEXANDRA

62. XIE KITCHIN as "A Chinaman"

63. PRINCE LEOPOLD, youngest son of Queen Victoria

64.   "St. George and the Dragon"

Notes on the Sitters and Plates

Negative numbers are given where stated by Lewis Carroll.

Ⅱⁿ stands for "second". It is made up of a Roman II combined with the loop of a "D" which contains a small "n". From time to time Lewis Carroll went through his stock of negatives, erasing some and filling the gaps in the numbers with new negatives, which were prefixed by this sign.

Dimensions do not refer to plate size but to the print, which is usually considerably cut down, since Lewis Carroll rarely used the plate to the full extent, and was fond of cutting his prints into fancy shapes—ovals, circles, and gothic. The horizontal dimension is given first.

The photographs have been dated according to entries in Lewis Carroll's diaries, and the Plates are arranged in chronological order.

With the exception of Plate 12, all photographs are in the Gernsheim Collection, University of Texas.

1. Lewis Carroll (The Rev. Charles Lutwidge Dodgson, M.A.)

THIS photograph of Lewis Carroll holding a lens shows the pride and pleasure he took in his hobby. On the back of the card he wrote "Done by Rejlander", which should dispel any idea that this is a self-portrait, as has been claimed elsewhere.

Lewis Carroll hated publicity and for this reason fought shy of being photographed; nevertheless, he had his portrait taken by several photographers besides Rejlander. He was photographed by Reginald Southey, a fellow Student, in 1856; by H. P. Robinson in 1857; by Dr. G. C. Wallich of London in 1866; by Hills & Saunders of Oxford in 1895. W. Shawcross, a Guildford photographer, took the last portrait of him in 1897.

Owing to the circumstance that Lewis Carroll re-photographed other photographers' portraits of him, omitting their names from his copies, I have only been able to identify those mentioned above.

Carte de visite. Taken on 28th March 1863 by O. G. Rejlander.

85

37. *The Rev. C. Barker and his daughter May*

Neg. No. 1233. 6″×8″. Taken on 6th June 1864 at Christ Church, Oxford. (See page 57.)

2. —— *Benn*

Neg. No. 116. 5⅜″×4″. Taken in July 1856 at Croft Rectory, Yorkshire. Contained in album No. VI.

27. *Helene Beyer*

A German model, who posed as "Joan of Arc" for Dante Gabriel Rossetti's oil painting and Alexander Munro's sculpture. William Michael Rossetti wrote, "She had one of the most classically correct and strongest profiles that one could see anywhere."
Neg. No. 1139. 4¾″×6⅜″. Autographed. Taken on 9th October 1863 at Rossetti's house, 16 Cheyne Walk, Chelsea. (See page 56.)

55. *Cyril Bickersteth*

Son of Robert Bickersteth, second Bishop of Ripon.
Neg. No. 1427. 4⅞″×6⅞″. Autographed. Taken on 7th September 1865 at Ripon Palace. (See page 63.)

54. *Florence Bickersteth*

Daughter of Robert Bickersteth, second Bishop of Ripon.
Neg. No. 1440. 4⅞″×7″. Autographed. Taken on 8th September 1865 at Ripon Palace. (See page 63.)

38. *Ivo Bligh*

Son of Lord Darnley.
Neg. No. 1293. 4″×5¾″. Autographed. Taken on 7th July 1864 at Lambeth Palace.

60. *Katie Brine*

Granddaughter of Dr. Pusey, Dean of Christ Church.
Neg. No. 1484. 3⅞″×5″. Autographed. Taken on 15th June 1866 at Christ Church, Oxford.

4. Coates

Daughter of one of the employees at Croft Rectory.
Neg. No. 287. $4\frac{3}{4}''\times6''$. Taken c. 1857. (See page 33.)

39. Grace Denman ("Little Dear")

Daughter of Lord Chief Justice Denman.
Neg. No. 1310. $5\frac{3}{8}''$ circle. Taken on 8th July 1864 at Lambeth Palace.

6. The Misses Dodgson and Edwin Dodgson

Six of Lewis Carroll's sisters and his youngest brother in the drawing-room at Croft Rectory.
$6\frac{1}{4}''\times4\frac{3}{4}''$. Taken c. 1857. (See page 33.)

7. Louisa, Margaret and Henrietta Dodgson

Lewis Carroll's three youngest sisters in the garden at Croft Rectory.
$5\frac{1}{4}''\times4''$. Taken c. 1857. Contained in album No. VI.

58. Alice Emily Donkin and Alice Jane Donkin

Alice Emily was a daughter of William Fishburn Donkin, F.R.S., Professor of Astronomy at Oxford. Her first cousin Alice Jane (see also Plate 15) married Wilfrid Dodgson, one of Lewis Carroll's brothers.
Neg. No. 1455. $3\frac{7}{8}''\times5''$. Taken on 14th May 1866 at Christ Church. Photograph entitled by Lewis Carroll "The Two Alices".

15. Alice Jane Donkin

$7\frac{1}{2}''\times9\frac{3}{4}''$. Taken at Barmby Moor, 9th October 1862. Photograph entitled by Lewis Carroll "The Elopement". (See page 51.) Neg No. ℙ 34.

52. Dymphna Ellis

Daughter of the Rector of Cranbourne, near Windsor.
Neg. No. 1378. $3\frac{5}{8}''\times4\frac{7}{8}''$. Autographed. Taken on 25th July 1865 at Cranbourne. (See page 62.)

44. Mrs. Franklin and her daughter Rose

Mrs. Franklin was the wife of the colonel commanding the fort near Freshwater.
Neg. No. ℙ42. $6''\times8''$. Taken on 15th August 1864 at Farringford. (See Lewis Carroll's letter to his sister, page 61.)

35. Frederick, Crown Prince of Denmark (1843-1912)

Son of Christian IX, and a brother of Queen Alexandra; later King Frederick VIII of Denmark. Was an undergraduate at Christ Church at the time this photograph was taken.

Neg. No. 1197. 6¼″×8″. Autographed, and dated 18th November 1863. Taken at Badcock's yard, Oxford. (See page 56.)

14. Beatrice Henley

Daughter of the Vicar at Putney. Her beauty may have inspired Lewis Carroll to write the poem "Beatrice" (see page 51).

Neg. No. ℗32. 3¾″×5⅛″. Autographed. Taken at Putney, September 1862.

32. Arthur Hughes and his daughter Agnes

Arthur Hughes (1832-1915) was a Pre-Raphaelite painter, though never a member of the Brotherhood.

Neg. No. 1177. 6″×8″. Autographed by Arthur Hughes, and dated 12th October 1863. Taken at George MacDonald's House, "Elm Lodge", Heath Street, Hampstead (see page 56).

33. Arthur Hughes Jr.

Son of Arthur Hughes.

Neg. No. 1171. 3¾″×4⅞″. Autographed. Taken on 12th October 1863.

29. Amy Hughes

Daughter of Arthur Hughes (Plate 32).

Neg. No. 1172. 3¾″×4⅞″. Taken on 12th October 1863.

36. Elizabeth Hussey

Daughter of Robert Hussey, Professor of Ecclesiastical History at Oxford. Neg. No. 1212. 5⅞″×4⅞″. Autographed. Taken on 26th April 1864 at Christ Church.

20. Marcus Keane

Neg. No. 1067. 4″×5⅜″. Taken at Whitby, 4th September 1863.

62. Alexandra (Xie) Kitchin as "A Chinaman"

Daughter of the Rev. George William Kitchin, Dean of Winchester and later of Durham. Queen Alexandra was godmother to her. She married Arthur Cardew.
Neg. No. 2155. Cabinet size. Taken on 14th July 1873 at Christ Church. (See page 70.) In the possession of Mrs. Bennett. The signature is taken from another photograph, in album No. III.

64. "St. George and the Dragon"

The models are Xie Kitchin and her brothers. Photographed at Christ Church about 1874. (See page 21.)

22. Alphonse Legros (1837-1911)

French painter and etcher. Professor of Etching at the Government Art Schools, South Kensington, and Slade Professor at London University.
Neg. No. 1128. 3⅞″×4⅞″. Autographed, and dated 1863. Taken at D. G. Rossetti's house, 16 Cheyne Walk, Chelsea, 6th October 1863. (See page 55.)

63. Prince Leopold (1853-84)

Queen Victoria's youngest son, when an Oxford undergraduate. Created Duke of Albany in 1881.
4⅞″×6⅞″. Autographed, and dated June 2, 1875. Taken at Christ Church. (See page 73.)

12. Alice Liddell (later Mrs. Reginald Hargreaves)

The original "Alice in Wonderland". Daughter of Henry George Liddell, Dean of Christ Church and Vice-Chancellor of Oxford University.
Taken in 1859, when Alice was seven years old. Lewis Carroll stuck this picture on the last page of the MS., *Alice's Adventures Under Ground* (see page 47). Reproduced by courtesy of the Trustees of the British Museum.

45. Alice Liddell

Photographed in the garden of the Deanery, Christ Church, 1859–60.

41. C. T. Longley (1794-1868)

Headmaster of Harrow School from 1829 to 1836, when he was nominated first Bishop of Ripon. In 1856 he became Bishop of Durham, in 1860 Archbishop of York and in 1862 Archbishop of Canterbury. Stuart Dodgson Collingwood wrote, "His charming character endeared him to the Archdeacon [Lewis Carroll's father] and his family, as to everyone else who saw much of him. He was one of the few men whose faces can truly be called *beautiful*." No doubt for this reason Lewis Carroll photographed him more often than any other man. Perhaps he also wanted to keep up to date with the successive stages of Longley's advancement, for Lewis Carroll loved contact with public figures.

Neg. No. 1304. $4\frac{3}{8}'' \times 5\frac{7}{8}''$. Signed as Archbishop of Canterbury at Lambeth Palace and dated July 8, 1864. (See page 58.)

11. The Misses Lutwidge

Two of Lewis Carroll's aunts.
Neg. No. 440. $6'' \times 7''$. Taken c. 1858.

30. George MacDonald and his daughter Lily

George MacDonald (1824-1905) was a Scottish novelist and poet. For three years a Congregational minister, he resigned owing to complaints that his sermons lacked doctrine. From then on he devoted himself solely to literature.

Lilia Scott MacDonald was the eldest of his family of eleven. She had a great talent for acting, and was introduced by Lewis Carroll to Mrs. Arthur Lewis (Kate Terry). Phelps admired her acting in private performances. She died of consumption at the age of thirty-nine at Bordighera, where the MacDonalds had a villa.

Neg. No. 1183. $6'' \times 8''$. Autographed by both. Taken on 14th October 1863. This and the other MacDonald photographs were taken at their house, "Elm Lodge", Heath Street, Hampstead. (See page 56.)

31. Greville MacDonald

Son of George MacDonald. Became a medical specialist, and published memoirs of his parents, and his own life.
Neg. No. 1165. $4'' \times 5\frac{3}{8}''$. Autographed. Taken on 10th October 1863.

16. Irene MacDonald

One of the eleven children of George MacDonald (Plate 30). She married Cecil Brewer, a well-known architect, in 1904.

Neg. No. 1027. 6″×8″. Taken in July 1863. Entitled by Lewis Carroll "It won't come smooth". This picture might almost serve to illustrate Lewis Carroll's poem "Those Horrid Hurdy-Gurdies" (1861):

> My mother bids me bind my hair,
> And not go about such a figure;
> It's a bother, of course, but what do I care?
> I shall do as I please when I'm bigger.

17. Irene MacDonald

Neg. No. 1008. 7⅜″×5½″. Autographed. Taken in July 1863.

28. Mary MacDonald

Mary and her brother Greville (Plate 31) were the first children of the MacDonald family with whom Lewis Carroll made friends. He met them in the winter 1860-61 at the studio of Alexander Munro (Plate 25), where Greville was posing for Munro's fountain in Hyde Park—a boy riding on a dolphin. Soon Lewis Carroll was "Uncle" to all the family. The enthusiastic reception given by the MacDonald children to *Alice's Adventures Under Ground* encouraged Lewis Carroll to publish the story, Greville setting the seal on this approval by declaring that there should be sixty thousand volumes of it.

Mary became engaged to Arthur Hughes's nephew, but died of consumption at the early age of twenty-four in 1878 at Nervi.

Neg. No. 1161. 3⅝″×4⅞″. Autographed. Taken on 10th October 1863.

48. (Sir) John Everett Millais (1829-96)

One of the three founder-members of the Pre-Raphaelite Brotherhood, he gradually grew away from the ideals which had first united them. In his desire to make a successful career he turned to popular subjects and fashionable portraits, reckoning on making £30,000 to £40,000 a year. He was created a baronet in 1885 and became President of the Royal Academy eleven years later.

Neg. No. 1366. 3¾″×4¾″. Autographed. Taken on 21st July 1865 at Millais's home. (See page 62.)

49. (Sir) John Everett Millais with his wife and daughters

As Effie Gray, she was Ruskin's "Fair Maid of Perth" and married him at

the age of 19. She posed for Millais's "The Order of Release", and later married him, her marriage with Ruskin having been annulled.
Neg. No. 1363. $3\frac{5}{8}''\times 4\frac{7}{8}''$. Taken on 21st July 1865. Autographed by Mrs. Millais. (See page 62.)

50. Effie Millais

Daughter of John Millais.
Neg. No. 1359. $3\frac{5}{8}''\times 4\frac{7}{8}''$. Autographed. Taken on 20th July 1865.

51. Mary Millais

Daughter of John Millais.
Neg. No. 1369. $3\frac{3}{4}''\times 4\frac{7}{8}''$. Autographed. Taken on 21st July 1865.

25. Alexander Munro and his wife

Alexander Munro (1825-71) was a sculptor, mainly in the field of portrait busts and medallions. He was a regular exhibitor at the Royal Academy from 1849 until his death. Lewis Carroll admired his work and photographed many of his sculptures. Munro introduced him to several important people: Tom Taylor, Arthur Hughes, D. G. Rossetti, Holman Hunt, Val Prinsep.
Neg. No. 1136. $4\frac{7}{8}''\times 5\frac{3}{8}''$. Taken at Rossetti's house in Chelsea, 7th October 1863. (See page 56.)

5. Alice Murdoch

One of Lewis Carroll's earliest photographs. The verses opposite the photograph in the album (see page 38) are in Lewis Carroll's handwriting, and· are probably by him.
Neg. No. 53. $3''\times 4''$. Taken at Putney on 19th June 1856. Contained in album No. VI.

40. Madeline Catherine Parnell

Niece of Mrs. Longley, wife of the Archbishop of Canterbury.
Neg. No. 1295. $2\frac{1}{2}''\times 3\frac{3}{8}''$. Autographed. Taken on 7th July 1864 at Lambeth Palace. (See page 58.)

61. John Phillips, F.R.S. (1800-74)

Professor of Geology at King's College, London; later at Trinity College, Dublin, and from 1853 at Oxford. Keeper of the Ashmolean Museum, 1854-70. President of the Geological Society.
Neg. No. 1501. $3\frac{5}{8}''\times 4\frac{7}{8}''$. Autographed, and dated July 11, 1866. Taken at Oxford.

34. Agnes Florence Price

Daughter of Bartholomew Price of Pembroke College, Professor of Natural Philosophy at Oxford.

Neg. No. 1203. $5'' \times 6\frac{1}{2}''$. Autographed. Taken on 2nd May 1864 at Oxford.

21. Dante Gabriel Rossetti (1828-82)

Equally celebrated as poet and painter; founder-member of the Pre-Raphaelite Brotherhood.

Neg. No. 1126. $4'' \times 5\frac{3}{8}''$. Autographed, and dated Oct 6 1863. (See page 55.)

23. Christina Rossetti and her mother, Frances Rossetti

Christina was born in 1830 and died in 1894. After Elizabeth Barrett Browning she was the leading poetess in England. She was exceedingly religious, and Lewis Carroll kept up his acquaintance with her until the close of her life, sending her his successive publications.

Neg. No. 1130. $3\frac{7}{8}'' \times 4\frac{7}{8}''$. Autographed by both. Taken on 7th October 1863. (See page 56.)

24. Dante Gabriel, Christina, William Michael and Mrs. Rossetti

William Michael Rossetti (1829-1919) was a member of the Pre-Raphaelite Brotherhood and editor of their short-lived journal *The Germ*. He was a man of letters and an art critic.

Neg. No. 1132. $7\frac{7}{8}'' \times 6\frac{3}{8}''$. Autographed by Dante Gabriel and William Michael Rossetti. Taken on 7th October 1863 at Tudor House, 16 Cheyne Walk, Chelsea, the home of Dante Gabriel and William Michael Rossetti and Algernon Swinburne. (See page 56.)

Lewis Carroll took all the Rossetti photographs at the same address, where he also photographed many of his friends. Another very similar group, taken on the same day, is in the author's collection. It shows Mrs. Rossetti playing chess with Dante Gabriel, and includes Christina, and her elder sister Maria Francesca, instead of William Michael Rossetti.

26. Zoë Strong

A relative of Dr. Thomas Banks Strong, Dean of Christ Church in 1901 and later Bishop of Oxford.

Neg. No. 1167. $3\frac{1}{4}'' \times 4\frac{1}{8}''$. Autographed. Taken at George MacDonald's house, 10th October 1863.

93

19. Tom Taylor (1817-80)

Barrister, dramatist and critic. Editor of *Punch* from 1874 until his death in 1880. It was he who introduced Lewis Carroll to the Terry family and Arthur Hughes.

Neg. No. 1111. 6″×8″. Autographed, and dated 3rd October 1863. Taken at Tom Taylor's home at Wandsworth. (See page 54.)

18. Wicliffe Taylor

Son of Tom Taylor.

Neg. No. 1122. 3⅞″×5″. Taken on 3rd October 1863 in the costume of a knight. (See page 54.)

8. Alfred, Lord Tennyson (1809-92)

Appointed Poet Laureate in 1850 in succession to Wordsworth. In 1884 he was raised to the peerage.

Lewis Carroll summed up his impression of the poet's appearance in the following words: "A strange shaggy-looking man; his hair, moustache and beard looked wild and neglected; these very much hid the character of the face. He was dressed in a loosely fitting morning coat, common grey flannel waistcoat and trousers, and a carelessly tied black silk neckerchief. His hair is black; and I think the eyes too; they are keen and restless—nose aquiline—forehead high and broad—both face and head are fine and manly. His manner was kind and friendly from the first; there is a dry lurking humour in his style of talking . . . "

7″×8¾″. Autograph cut out from a letter to Lewis Carroll. Taken on 28th September 1857 at Coniston in the Lake District, where the Tennysons were staying for a summer holiday (see page 42). On the same day Lewis Carroll took another portrait of Tennyson in a different pose. This is illustrated in *Life and Letters of Lewis Carroll* by S. D. Collingwood, 1898, page 70.

9. Hallam Tennyson (1852-1928)

Elder son of Lord Tennyson; became second baron. Governor-General of Australia 1902-04; wrote a biography of his father.

3⅞″×5⅛″. Taken at Coniston, 28th September 1857.

47. (Dame) Ellen Terry (1847-1928)

Famous actress. Her first husband was G. F. Watts, the painter, whom she married in 1864. Lewis Carroll admired her on her first appearance on the stage, as Mamillius in *The Winter's Tale* at the Princess's Theatre, London, in 1856. He did not make her acquaintance until April 1865. The two soon became good friends, and Ellen and her sisters Kate and Marion helped many of Lewis Carroll's child friends who wanted to take up acting as a profession.

After seeing Ellen Terry's performance as Ophelia he wrote:

> Empress of Art, for thee I twine
> This wreath with all too slender skill,
> Forgive my Muse each halting line,
> And for the deed accept the will!

Neg. No. 1339. $2\frac{1}{2}'' \times 3\frac{3}{8}''$. Autographed with her married name. Taken on 14th July 1865, at the Terrys' home in Kentish Town, London (see page 62), where Lewis Carroll photographed every member of the large Terry family, except the baby Fred.

46. Marion Terry ("Polly") and Florence Maud Terry ("Flo")

Younger sisters of Ellen Terry, both successful actresses.
Neg. No. 1341. $3\frac{5}{8}'' \times 4\frac{7}{8}''$. Entitled by Lewis Carroll "Polly and Flo". Autographed by Polly. Taken on 14th July 1865. (See page 62.)

10. Agnes Grace Weld

Mrs. Tennyson's niece. This, and another photograph of the same child, formed Lewis Carroll's means of introduction to the Tennysons. (See p. 42.) $5\frac{1}{2}'' \times 3\frac{3}{4}''$. Entitled by Lewis Carroll "Little Red Riding-hood". Taken at Croft Rectory, 18th August 1857. Together with three other photographs, Lewis Carroll exhibited "Little Red Riding-hood" at the fifth exhibition of the Photographic Society, held at the South Kensington Museum in 1858. It is No. 174 in the exhibition catalogue. (See page 42.)

13. Agnes Grace Weld

See 10.
$4\frac{1}{2}'' \times 6''$. Taken *c.* 1861.

42. Alice Constance Westmacott

Daughter of the sculptor Richard Westmacott.
Neg. No. 1316. $3\frac{3}{4}'' \times 4\frac{7}{8}''$. Autographed. Taken on 9th July 1864 at Lambeth Palace.

43. Maria White

Niece of the porter at Lambeth Palace.
Neg. No. ℙ9. $3\frac{7}{8}'' \times 4\frac{7}{8}''$. Autographed. Taken on 11th July 1864 at Lambeth Palace.

59. Ella C. F. Williams

Daughter of Sir Monier Monier-Williams, Professor of Sanskrit at Oxford. She married the Rev. Samuel Bickersteth.
$3\frac{7}{8}'' \times 5''$. Autographed. Taken on 24th May 1866 at Oxford. (See page 63.)

53. Aileen Wilson-Todd

Neg. No. 1416. $3\frac{3}{4}'' \times 4\frac{3}{4}''$. Autographed. Taken on 4th September 1865 at Croft Rectory.

56. Charlotte M. Yonge and her mother, Frances Mary Yonge

Neg. No. 1453. $3\frac{7}{8}'' \times 5''$. Autographed by both, and dated 4th May 1866. (See page 64.)

57. Charlotte M. Yonge (1823-1901)

Novelist. The most famous of her 160 books was *The Heir of Redclyffe*, which reached twenty-two editions by 1875. She also wrote some books for children. Edited *The Monthly Packet* for over thirty-eight years. Lewis Carroll's *A Tangled Tale* appeared in it serially, starting in April 1880. She taught Scripture daily in the village school, went to service twice a day, devoted all the proceeds of her books to good causes. She had to submit each day's writing to her parents for criticism.
Neg. No. 1452. $3\frac{1}{8}'' \times 4\frac{1}{8}''$. Autographed and dated 4th May 1866. Taken at Badcock's yard. (See page 64.)

3. Three girls (unnamed)

Three young girls sitting on the lawn.
$6\frac{3}{4}'' \times 3\frac{3}{8}''$. Taken at Croft Rectory *c.* 1857.

Important dates in the life of the
Rev. Charles Lutwidge Dodgson, M.A.
("Lewis Carroll")

27th Jan. 1832   Born at Daresbury, Cheshire, the eldest son of the Rev. Charles Dodgson.

1843   Moved to Croft Rectory, Yorkshire.

1844-1846   Educated at Richmond, Yorkshire.

1846-1849   Educated at Rugby.

23rd May 1850   Matriculated at Christ Church, Oxford.

24th Jan. 1851   Entered into residence at Christ Church, where he lived until his death.

24th Dec. 1852   Nominated Student of Christ Church. No definite work was entailed in the Studentship, to which two conditions were attached: that the Student should remain unmarried and should proceed to Holy Orders.

Jan. 1856   Became mathematical lecturer.

March 1856   First use of the pseudonym "Lewis Carroll" under the poem *Solitude*, published in *The Train: a First-class Magazine*, Vol. 1, p. 154. "Lewis" was derived via Ludovicus (Lat.) from Lutwidge; "Carroll" via Carolus (Lat.) from Charles.

1857   Master of Arts.

22nd Dec. 1861   Ordained deacon.

July 1865   Publication of *Alice's Adventures in Wonderland*.

End of 1871   Publication of *Through the Looking-Glass and What Alice Found There*.

March 1876   Publication of *The Hunting of the Snark*.

18th Oct. 1881   Resigned mathematical lectureship.

14th Jan. 1898   Died at his sisters' home in Guildford, Surrey.

Chronology of Lewis Carroll's Photography

8th Sept. 1855   Interest aroused by watching his uncle photographing.

18th Sept. 1855   Wrote *Photography Extraordinary*, first published Nov. 3rd 1855—periodical unknown.

18th Mar. 1856   Ordered photographic outfit.

3rd June 1856   Took his first successful photographs.

13th Nov. 1857   Finished *Hiawatha's Photographing*, first published in *The Train*, December 1857.

February 1858   Showed four photographs at the fifth exhibition of the Photographic Society of London.

Bet. 1858-1860   Wrote *The Legend of "Scotland"*, which contains *The Ladye's History*.

1860   *A Photographer's Day Out* published in the *South Shields Amateur Magazine*.

1860 or early in 1861   *Photographs*, a list published for private circulation.

May 1863   Rented Badcock's yard, Oxford, for photographing.

16th Mar. 1872   Took first photograph in specially constructed "glass-house" over his rooms at Christ Church.

15th July 1880   Last entry in diary relating to taking photographs.

Lewis Carroll's Photograph Albums

LIKE all Victorians, Lewis Carroll was an ardent collector of photographs. The auction of his personal effects soon after his death included the astonishing number of thirty-three photograph albums. Unfortunately, the sale catalogue makes no distinction between albums of collected photographs and those containing his own work, but in view of the fact that the highest numbered album which I have been able to trace—No. X—consists chiefly of professional photographs, I think we are justified in assuming that the remaining twenty-three were filled with the usual *carte-de-visite* and cabinet portraits.

In collecting photographs of celebrities, Lewis Carroll manifests a strange inconsistency, for he himself could seldom be induced to give his *carte* to grown-ups, and seems to have insisted, on the rare occasions when he sat to a professional photographer, that his portrait should not be sold to the public, like those of other celebrities. "My reason is that I want to be personally unknown: to be known by sight by strangers would be intolerable to me." Lewis Carroll's *carte* is therefore very rarely to be found in the usual Victorian photograph album, and his attitude was no doubt a great disappointment to the photographers concerned, since the potential demand was very large.

Scrupulous to the point of being pedantic in everything he did, it is the more curious that, quite unwittingly, Lewis Carroll more than once infringed the Copyright Act of 1862 by reproducing other photographers' portraits of him and making his own *carte-de-visite* or cabinet prints from these, which he would present to child friends in exchange for their pictures, which afterwards adorned his albums.

> Your picture shall adorn the book
> That's bound so neatly and moroccoly,
> With that bright green which every cook
> Delights to see in beds of cauliflower.
>
> The *carte* is very good, but pray
> Send me the larger one as well!
> "A cool request!" I hear you say,
> "Give him an inch, he takes an acre!"

When Lewis Carroll sent Maggie Cunnynghame a comic sketch of himself on January 30th 1868, he accompanied it by a letter in verse, part of which runs—

No *carte* has yet been done of me
That does real justice to my *smile*;
And so I hardly like, you see,
To send you one—however, I'll
Consider if I will or not . . .

Later on he sent the *carte* but Maggie did not like it, so he teased her again (April 7th 1868):

" . . . Oh Maggie, how *can* you ask for a better one of me than the one I sent! It is one of the best ever done! Such grace, such dignity, such benevolence, such— As a great secret (please don't repeat it), the Queen sent to ask for a copy of it, but as it is against my rule to give in such a case, I was obliged to answer—'Mr. Dodgson presents his compliments to her Majesty, and regrets to say that his rule is never to give his photograph except to *young* ladies.' I am told she was annoyed about it, and said, 'I'm not so old as all that comes to!' and one doesn't like to annoy Queens; but really I couldn't help it, you know."

Of the albums containing Lewis Carroll's own photographs I have been able to trace twelve. However, there are gaps in the numbered albums, and the omission to number others is unaccountable unless he had given them away before he did the numbering and indexing of albums in August 1875. But this is only a surmise, for Lewis Carroll was by no means as methodical and logical as one would expect. It seems to go against all reason to give one's first album the number VI, and to prepare an index which does not tally with the contents!

According to diary entries of June 16th and 17th 1880, only a month before giving up his hobby, Lewis Carroll prepared a catalogue of all his photographs, which has to this day not been seen or heard of by anyone. Perhaps it would prove a source of information about the albums; but maybe it wouldn't—there is no knowing with Lewis Carroll. The catalogue was apparently not regarded as of sufficient value by his executors to be included in the sale of his effects in 1898. No wonder: the photograph albums themselves fetched only an average of eight shillings![1]

---

[1] What happened to Lewis Carroll's cameras, negatives, etc., which were disposed of at the same sale, is not known to me. Two copies of the first edition (1865) of *Alice's Adventures*

Before listing the albums—and I shall take the numbered ones first—I should mention that [A] stands for "album" and is always prefixed to the number, on the inside front cover. Lewis Carroll always wrote the number, index (when it exists) and page numbers in his favourite purple ink. Except when otherwise mentioned, the albums are bound in green cloth, half calf.

[A] I Entitled *Photographic Scrap Book* in gilt on front cover. Size 10¾×9¾ inches. Indexed. Contains 96 photographs, a few supposed not to be Lewis Carroll's work. Of the 65 portraits, 10 are of his family, 7 of the Liddell children with autographs, 4 of the Tennyson family with autographs, and Bishop Longley, autographed. The rest of the portraits are of other friends. 31 photographs are of views, pictures of skeletons, and of "Tim", the old family doll. *M. L. Parrish Collection, Princeton University, U.S.A.*

[A] II Entitled *Photographic Scrap Book Vol. II* in gilt on front cover. Size 11¼×9¾ inches. Indexed. Contains 136 photographs, all by Lewis Carroll. All except 12 are portraits, many autographed. On the first page is the autograph of the Prince of Wales—"Albert Edward P., Frewen Hall, Oxford. December 15th, 1860" but no photograph. Among the portraits of important people are the Bishops of Oxford, Ripon and Lincoln, J. Holman Hunt, George MacDonald, Thomas Woolner, Aubrey de Vere, Sir Michael Hicks-Beach, Dr. (Sir Henry) Acland, the Earl of Enniskillen, Professors Faraday, Dindorf, Brodie and Donkin. The remainder of the photographs are mostly of relations and friends, including many children (8 of the Liddells). There are 12 views, two of Daresbury Parsonage, one of Christ Church Deanery and garden. The album also contains a portrait of Lewis Carroll taken about 1860. Chiefly photographs of his best period. *M. L. Parrish Collection, Princeton University, U.S.A.*

[A] III Entitled *Photographs Vol. III* in gilt on front cover. Size 10½×11½ inches. Indexed. The negative numbers range from 955 to 1545. Contains 115 photographs, all by Lewis Carroll. All portraits except two—of Tom Quad with the new belfry at Christ Church, and a view of Farringford. The portraits are nearly all autographed, and include such celebrities as D.G. and Christina Rossetti, Charlotte M. Yonge, George MacDonald, Tom Taylor,

---

in Wonderland fetched only £24 and £50, as compared with Sir R. Leicester Harmsworth's first edition which was sold at Sotheby's in 1947 for £1,200, and the Earl of Harewood's copy, which reached at Christie's exactly one hundred years after its first publication £4,200.

Kate and Ellen Terry, Millais, Arthur Hughes, Alphonse Legros, Alexander Munro, Crown Prince Frederick of Denmark, Prince Leopold (Duke of Albany), Archbishop Longley, the Bishop of Ripon. The remainder are mostly of children, with their signatures, and since the illustrations in this book have been taken chiefly from this album a further description is unnecessary. It should be mentioned that the album has 140 numbered pages, several of which bear only the autograph of the sitter (e.g. Lord Salisbury and George Peabody). In some cases the photographs were omitted for unknown reasons; in others they were definitely failures. The photographs are of Lewis Carroll's best period. The album was formerly in the possession of Charlotte Yonge, whose name and address are entered on the inside back cover. *Gernsheim Collection, University of Texas.*

[A] VI Size 10½ × 7¼ inches. Inscribed in Lewis Carroll's handwriting on the inside front cover "Begun July 1856". This is his first album, in spite of its number. It contains an indexed list of 58 photographs, but actually there are 70. Negative numbers range from 41 to 294. The photographs are chiefly portraits of the Dodgson family and their friends; none are autographed. There are also some views of Croft Rectory, of Whitby, and of the Lake District, some reproductions of engravings, and a close-up of a kitten. *Gernsheim Collection, University of Texas.*

[A] VII Size 10½ × 7¼ inches. The index goes up to No. 60 but the album contains only 33 photographs. Some pages bear the sitter's signature but no picture. Negative numbers range from 159 to 752. All are portraits of members of Christ Church Common Room, and practically all are autographed. Includes portraits of Reginald Southey and Quintin Twiss. The only sitters who became well known are Henry Parry Liddon, Max Müller and Lewis Carroll himself (reading a book, with an out-of-focus garden background) — probably the portrait taken by Southey in 1856. Some are dated 1860, some 1862. Rather uninteresting photographs on the whole. *Christ Church Library, Oxford.*

[A] X Entitled *Professional and Other Photographs* in gilt on front cover. Size 12¼ × 14¾ inches. No index, pages not numbered. No photograph is autographed. Contains about six photographs by Lewis Carroll out of a total of 53. Among famous sitters are Alfred Tennyson (with autograph cut out from a letter), George MacDonald, Michael Faraday, Sir Henry Taylor and Hallam Tennyson. By far the largest proportion of the photographs is by O. G. Rejlander. Some of these are portraits, some studies for artists to paint from, and some exquisite photographs of children. In addition there are a number of portraits of well-known people by a professional photographer,

102

Herbert Watkins of Regent Street, London, three early studies by Julia Margaret Cameron, and an extraordinary collection of miscellaneous photographs ranging from the Stockport to Darlington locomotive, 1825, to a reproduction of Millais' "Apple Blossoms", and an engraving of an exceedingly sentimental Spanish Madonna and child painting. The main interest in this album lies in Lewis Carroll's choice of photographs which he considered worth collecting, revealing a not very discriminating taste. *Gernsheim Collection, University of Texas.*

UNNUMBERED ALBUMS

Album size 10×7 inches, not numbered or indexed. Contains 76 photographs, chiefly of the Dodgson family and their friends. None are autographed. It is very similar in contents to album No. VI, and presumably also dates from 1856 or 1857. The portraits are still very straightforward, lacking the originality and charm of later work. This album contains "Little Red Riding-hood" and the group of six of Lewis Carroll's sisters and his brother Edwin. *Gernsheim Collection, University of Texas.*

Album size $7\frac{1}{4} \times 8\frac{3}{4}$ inches, bound in dark green morocco leather, apparently given to Agnes Grace Weld or her mother, but not bearing any inscription. No index, pages not numbered. Contains 10 photographs by Lewis Carroll —of Agnes Grace Weld, her father, Hallam Tennyson, and various friends of the Welds. All early photographs, taken at Croft and Coniston in August and September 1857. *Gernsheim Collection, University of Texas.*

Album size $8\frac{1}{2} \times 11$ inches. No index. It contains 44 photographs of Christ Church undergraduates, none autographed. Almost without exception the sitters are taken in a leather-covered armchair in a stereotyped pose: rather immature work on the whole, certainly not equal to album No. VII. Dated February 1859 by its former owner, Charles M. Harvey, Christ Church. *Christ Church Library.*

Album entitled *Photographs* in gilt on front cover. Size $10\frac{3}{4} \times 9\frac{3}{4}$ inches. Indexed. Contains 94 photographs, 10 of which are views of Daresbury Parsonage, Croft Rectory, etc.; the remainder being portraits of the Dodgson family, their friends, and servants at Croft, also a number of celebrities including J. Holman Hunt, Millais, Tennyson, George MacDonald, Charlotte M. Yonge, the Crown Prince of Denmark, Prince Leopold (Duke of Albany), Lord Salisbury, Archbishop Longley and the Bishops of Oxford, Lincoln and Ripon. Only those of Longley and Holman Hunt are autographed. Chiefly work of Lewis Carroll's best period. *M. L. Parrish Collection, Princeton University, U.S.A.*

Album size $11\frac{1}{2} \times 10\frac{1}{4}$ inches. Bound in full leather. Bears the following inscription in Lewis Carroll's handwriting: "To Henry Holiday, in memory of a pleasant week spent with him in the Summer of 1875, this collection of amateur Photographs, taken during that visit, is presented by his sincere Friend C. L. Dodgson." Contains 24 photographs. Index and legend under each photograph are in Lewis Carroll's handwriting. *Princeton University, U.S.A.*

Album oblong quarto, entitled *Photographic Album* in gilt on front cover. No index. Contains 40 photographs, including Sir Frederick Gore-Ouseley, Dr. Corfe, Father R. M. Benson, Canon H. P. Liddon and Lewis Carroll himself. Exhibited at the Lewis Carroll Centenary Exhibition, London, 1932. *Then in the possession of Mrs. Prince, Farthinghoe.*

Distinguished Men and Women
Photographed by Lewis Carroll

(with cross-references to diary entries)

Artists	Arthur Hughes (p. 53)	1863
	Henry Holiday (p. 68)	1870
	J. Holman Hunt	1864 & 1872
	Alphonse Legros (p. 55)	1863
	(Sir) John Everett Millais (p. 6 2)	1865
	Alexander Munro (p. 53)	1863
	D. G. Rossetti (p. 55)	1863
	J. Sant (p. 65)	1866
	Thomas Woolner	1860
Writers and	George MacDonald (p. 53)	1863
Poets	Christina Rossetti (p. 55)	1863
	William Michael Rossetti (p. 56)	1863
	John Ruskin (p. 73)	1875
	Sir Henry Taylor (p. 51)	1862
	Tom Taylor (p. 53)	1863
	Alfred, Lord Tennyson (p. 42)	1857
	Aubrey de Vere (p. 51)	1862
	Charlotte M. Yonge (p. 64)	1866
Churchmen	Dr. C. T. Longley, Archbishop of Canterbury	
	(p. 58)	1864
	Dr. A. C. Tait, Archbishop of York (p. 79)	1880
	Dr. John Jackson, Bishop of Lincoln	1860
	Dr. Robert Bickersteth, Bishop of Ripon (p. 63)	1865
	Canon Edward King, afterwards Bishop of	
	Lincoln	1875
	Dr. Samuel Wilberforce, Bishop of Oxford	1860
	Dean Liddon (p. 65)	1867
	Dean Stanley	1860
	Rev. Frederick Denison Maurice (p. 53)	1863

Scientists	Sir Henry Acland (p. 38)	1856
	William Fishburn Donkin	1866
	Michael Faraday	1860
	Prof. John Phillips	1866
Professors	Friedrich Max Müller (p. 65)	1867
	Sir Frederick Gore-Ouseley	1860
	Bartholomew Price	1860
	Sir Monier Monier-Williams (p. 63)	1866
Actresses	Ellen Terry (p. 61)	1865
	Kate Terry (p. 61)	1865
	Marion Terry (p. 61)	1865
Politicians and Others	Sir Michael Hicks-Beach, M.P.	1862
	Earl of Enniskillen	1860
	Frederick, Crown Prince of Denmark, later King Frederick VIII (p. 56)	1863
	Prince Leopold, Duke of Albany (p. 73)	1875
	Sir John Mowbray, M.P. (p. 70)	1874
	George Peabody (p. 65)	1867
	Lord Salisbury (p. 67)	1870

In addition, Lewis Carroll tried to obtain sittings from the following: W. M. Thackeray (p. 40), the Prince of Wales (p. 46), Robert Browning (p. 54), G. F. Watts (p. 58), Princess Beatrice (p. 58), and Cardinal Newman (p. 79).

Bibliography

Lewis Carroll's diaries:
(No. 1 Lost.)
No. 2 January 1855 to September 1855.
(No. 3 Lost.)
No. 4 1st January 1856 to 31st December 1856.
No. 5 1st January 1857 to 17th April 1858.
(No. 6 Lost.)[1]
(No. 7 Lost.)[1]
No. 8 9th May 1862 to 6th September 1864.
No. 9 13th September 1864 to 24th January 1868.
No. 10 2nd April 1868 to 31st December 1876.
No. 11 1st January 1877 to 30th June 1883.
No. 12 1st July 1883 to 30th June 1892.
No. 13 1st July 1892 to 23rd December 1897.

The Complete Works of Lewis Carroll, with an introduction by Alexander Wooll-cott. Nonesuch Press, London, 1939.

Ethel M. Arnold: "Reminiscences of Lewis Carroll." *Windsor Magazine*, London, Christmas number, 1929.

Isa Bowman: *The Story of Lewis Carroll Told for Young People by the Real Alice in Wonderland*. London, 1899.

Stuart Dodgson Collingwood: *The Life and Letters of Lewis Carroll*. London, 1898. *The Lewis Carroll Picture Book*. London, 1899. "Before Alice: the Boyhood of Lewis Carroll." *Strand Magazine*, London, 1898, xvi, 616-27. "Some of Lewis Carroll's Child Friends; with Unpublished Letters by the Author of 'Alice in Wonderland'." *Century Magazine*, New York, April 1899.

C. L. Dodgson: "A Visit to Tennyson." *Strand Magazine*, London, May 1901 (published posthumously).

Caryl Hargreaves: "Alice's Recollections of Carrollian Days, Told by her Son." *Cornhill Magazine*, London, July 1932, pp.1-12.

---

[1] See Preface to the Dover Edition.

107

Beatrice Hatch: "Lewis Carroll." *Strand Magazine*, London, 1898, xv, 212-23.

Evelyn M. Hatch: *A Selection from the Letters of Lewis Carroll to his Child Friends*. London, 1933.

Florence Becker Lennon: *Lewis Carroll: a Biography*. London, 1947.

E. V. Lucas: "Charles Lutwidge Dodgson." Article in the Dictionary of National Biography, Supplement II, London, 1901.

Langford Reed: *The Life of Lewis Carroll*. London, 1932.

"E. L. S.": "Lewis Carroll as Artist, and Other Oxford Memoirs." *Cornhill Magazine*, London, November 1932.

"Lewis Carroll as Photographer." An 8-page supplement to *Lilliput*, London, July, 1940. Includes a photograph of the original Alice in Wonderland, but the attribution of the other six photographs to Lewis Carroll is almost certainly wrong.

A Catalogue of the Furniture, Personal Effects and Library of the Late Lewis Carroll (Rev. C. L. Dodgson, M.A.), author of "Alice in Wonderland", sold by auction at Holywell Music Room, Oxford, on Tuesday, May 10th, and following days. Oxford, 1898.

Lewis Carroll: 1832-1932. Catalogue of an exhibition to commemorate the hundredth anniversary of the birth of Lewis Carroll. Avery Library, Columbia University, 1932.

Falconer Madan: *The Lewis Carroll Centenary Exhibition Catalogue*. London, 1932.

Morris L. Parrish: *List of the Writings of Lewis Carroll in the Library at Dormy House, Pine Valley, New Jersey, collected by Morris L. Parrish*. Printed for private circulation. Part III, 1928.

Alvin Langdon Coburn: "The Old Masters of Photography." *Century Magazine*, New York, 1915, vol. xc.

Harry Furniss: *The Confessions of a Caricaturist*, Vol. 1. London, 1901.

Greville M. MacDonald: *George MacDonald and his Wife*. London, 1924.

Ellen Terry: *The Story of My Life*. London, 1908.

LEWIS CARROLL'S WRITINGS ON PHOTOGRAPHY

I

Photography Extraordinary

Photography Extraordinary is contained in *Misch-Masch*, one of Lewis Carroll's family magazines, which consisted largely of printed stories and verses he had written for *The Oxonian Advertiser, The Whitby Gazette* and other papers, besides some unpublished material. The story was written on 18th September 1855, but where it was first published could not be ascertained. Unfortunately the title of the journal does not appear on the cutting which Lewis Carroll inserted in *Misch-Masch*. The entry in his diary merely reads "Inserted in No. 13, Nov. 3 1855". *Misch-Masch* is now, like Lewis Carroll's earlier family magazine *The Rectory Umbrella*, in the Amory Collection, Harvard University, U.S.A.

THE recent extraordinary discovery in Photography, as applied to the operations of the mind, has reduced the art of Novel-writing to the merest mechanical labour. We have been kindly permitted by the artist to be present during one of his experiments, but as the invention has not yet been given to the world, we are only at liberty to relate the results, suppressing all details of chemicals and manipulation.

The operator began by stating that the ideas of the feeblest intellect, when once received on properly prepared paper, could be "developed" up to any required degree of intensity. On hearing our wish that he would begin with an extreme case, he obligingly summoned a young man from an adjoining room, who appeared to be of the very weakest possible physical and mental powers. On being asked what we thought of him we candidly confessed that he seemed incapable of anything but sleep; our friend cordially assented to this opinion.

The machine being in position, and a mesmeric rapport established between the mind of the patient and the object glass, the young man was asked whether he wished to say anything; he feebly replied "Nothing". He was then asked what he was thinking of, and the answer, as before, was "Nothing". The artist on this pronounced him to be in a most satisfactory state, and at once commenced the operation.

110

After the paper had been exposed for the requisite time, it was removed and submitted to our inspection; we found it to be covered with faint and almost illegible characters. A closer scrutiny revealed the following:

"The eve was soft and dewy mild; a zephyr whispered in the lofty glade, and a few light drops of rain cooled the thirsty soil. At a slow amble, along the primrose-bordered path rode a gentle-looking and amiable youth, holding a light cane in his delicate hand; the pony moved gracefully beneath him, inhaling as it went the fragrance of the roadside flowers; the calm smile, and languid eyes, so admirably harmonizing with the fair features of the rider, showed the even tenor of his thoughts. With a sweet though feeble voice, he plaintively murmured out the gentle regrets that clouded his breast:

'Alas! she would not hear my prayer!
Yet it were rash to tear my hair;
Disfigured, I should be less fair.

'She was unwise, I may say blind;
Once she was lovingly inclined;
Some circumstance has changed her mind.'

There was a moment's silence; the pony stumbled over a stone in the path, and unseated his rider. A crash was heard among the dried leaves; the youth arose; a slight bruise on his left shoulder, and a disarrangement of his cravat, were the only traces that remained of this trifling accident."

"This", we remarked, as we returned the paper, "belongs apparently to the milk-and-water School of Novels."

"You are quite right", our friend replied, "and, in its present state, it is, of course, utterly unsaleable in the present day: we shall find, however, that the next stage of development will remove it into the strong-minded or Matter-of-Fact School." After dipping it into various acids, he again submitted it to us; it had now become the following:

"The evening was of the ordinary character, barometer at 'change', a wind was getting up in the wood, and some rain was beginning to fall; a bad look-out for the farmers. A gentleman approached along the bridle-road, carrying a stout knobbed stick in his hand, and mounted on a serviceable nag, possibly worth some £40 or so; there was a settled business-like expression on the rider's face, and he whistled as he rode; he seemed to be hunting for rhymes in his head, and at length repeated, in a satisfied tone, the following composition:

'Well! so my offer was no go!
She might do worse, I told her so;
She was a fool to answer "No".

111

'However, things are as they stood;
Nor would I have her if I could,
For there are plenty more as good.'

At this moment the horse set his foot in a hole, and rolled over; his rider rose with difficulty; he had sustained several severe bruises and fractured two ribs; it was some time before he forgot that unlucky day."

We returned this with the strongest expression of admiration, and requested that it might now be developed to the highest possible degree. Our friend readily consented, and shortly presented us with the result, which he informed us belonged to the Spasmodic or German School. We perused it with indescribable sensations of surprise and delight:

"The night was wildly tempestuous—a hurricane raved through the murky forest—furious torrents of rain lashed the groaning earth. With a headlong rush—down a precipitous mountain gorge—dashed a mounted horseman armed to the teeth—his horse bounded beneath him at a mad gallop, snorting fire from its distended nostrils as it flew. The rider's knotted brows—rolling eyeballs—and clenched teeth—expressed the intense agony of his mind—weird visions loomed upon his burning brain—while with a mad yell he poured forth the torrent of his boiling passion:

'Firebrands and daggers! hope hath fled!
To atoms dash the doubly dead!
My brain is fire—my heart is lead!

'Her soul is flint, and what am I?
Scorch'd by her fierce, relentless eye.
Nothingness is my destiny!'

There was a moment's pause. Horror! his path ended in a fathomless abyss ... A rush—a flash—a crash—all was over. Three drops of blood, two teeth, and a stirrup were all that remained to tell where the wild horseman met his doom."

The young man was now recalled to consciousness, and shown the result of the workings of his mind; he instantly fainted away.

In the present infancy of the art we forbear from further comment on this wonderful discovery; but the mind reels as it contemplates the stupendous addition thus made to the powers of science.

Our friend concluded with various minor experiments, such as working up a passage of Wordsworth into strong, sterling poetry: the same experiment was tried on a passage of Byron, at our request, but the paper came out scorched and blistered all over by the fiery epithets thus produced.

112

As a concluding remark: *could* this art be applied (we put the question in the strictest confidence)—*could* it, we ask, be applied to the speeches in Parliament? It may be but a delusion of our heated imagination, but we will still cling fondly to the idea, and hope against hope.

II

Hiawatha's Photographing

Hiawatha's Photographing was finished on November 13th 1857 and first appeared in *The Train*, December 1857. It was republished in *Phantasmagoria and Other Poems* (1869) and in *Rhyme? and Reason?* (1883) with six illustrations by A. B. Frost.

The three publications of this parody listed above all differ from one another. Not wishing to turn my book into a literary exercise by either entering into lengthy explanations of all the omissions, additions and alterations occurring in the three versions, or by printing all three side by side—and this alone would make the many differences quite clear to the reader—I reprint the parody in its final and most polished form as contained in *Rhyme? and Reason?* (1883), which is, incidentally, also the version accepted by Alexander Woollcott in *The Complete Works of Lewis Carroll* (1939).

At first sight one may be astonished by the many differences to be found in the three successive publications of this poem in Lewis Carroll's lifetime. He was, of course, activated by several motives in addition to the artist's natural desire to polish and re-polish his work. Feeling that to give detailed descriptions of all the members of the family who sat for their photograph was rather overdoing the joke, he omitted the two younger daughters from the version printed in *Phantasmagoria and Other Poems* and shortened the description of their father's contemplation. Lewis Carroll added on the one hand the six lines at the end (beginning "Hurriedly he packed his boxes"), which are also retained in the last version, printed here. On the other hand, he deleted from this version the eighteen lines about photographic manipulation quoted below, for much of this had become obsolete with the widespread introduction of the dry plate in 1880.

> First, a piece of glass he coated
> With collodion, and plunged it
> In a bath of lunar caustic

113

Carefully dissolved in water—
There he left it certain minutes.
   Secondly, my Hiawatha
Made with cunning hand a mixture
Of the acid pyrro-gallic,
And of glacial-acetic,
And of alcohol and water—
This developed all the picture.
   Finally, he fixed each picture
With a saturate solution
Which was made of hyposulphite,
Which, again, was made of soda.
(Very difficult the name is
For a metre like the present
But periphrasis has done it.)

In Lewis Carroll's opinion, Longfellow was "the greatest living master of language," and in this parody of *The Song of Hiawatha* he describes the worries and troubles of a photographer, no doubt drawing to a large extent upon his own experience. He introduces his parody with a note written in the same metre but printed as prose.

(IN AN age of imitation, I can claim no special merit for this slight attempt at doing what is known to be so easy. Any fairly practised writer, with the slightest ear for rhythm, could compose, for hours together, in the easy running metre of *The Song of Hiawatha*. Having, then, distinctly stated that I challenge no attention in the following little poem to its merely verbal jingle, I must beg the candid reader to confine his criticism to its treatment of the subject.)

From his shoulder Hiawatha
Took the camera of rosewood,
Made of sliding, folding rosewood;
Neatly put it all together.
In its case it lay compactly,
Folded into nearly nothing;
But he opened out the hinges,
Pushed and pulled the joints and hinges,
Till it looked all squares and oblongs,
Like a complicated figure
In the Second Book of Euclid.
   This he perched upon a tripod—
Crouched beneath its dusky cover—
Stretched his hand, enforcing silence—
Said, "Be motionless, I beg you!"
Mystic, awful was the process.
   All the family in order

Sat before him for their pictures:
Each in turn as he was taken,
Volunteered his own suggestions,
His ingenious suggestions.

First the Governor, the Father:
He suggested velvet curtains
Looped about a massy pillar;
And the corner of a table,
Of a rosewood dining-table.
He would hold a scroll of something,
Hold it firmly in his left-hand;
He would keep his right-hand buried
(Like Napoleon) in his waistcoat;
He would contemplate the distance
With a look of pensive meaning,
As of ducks that die in tempests.

Grand, heroic was the notion:
Yet the picture failed entirely:
Failed, because he moved a little,
Moved, because he couldn't help it.

Next, his better half took courage;
She would have her picture taken.
She came dressed beyond description,
Dressed in jewels and in satin
Far too gorgeous for an empress.
Gracefully she sat down sideways,
With a simper scarcely human,
Holding in her hand a bouquet
Rather larger than a cabbage.
All the while that she was sitting,
Still the lady chattered, chattered,
Like a monkey in the forest.
"Am I sitting still?" she asked him.
"Is my face enough in profile?
Shall I hold the bouquet higher?
Will it come into the picture?"
And the picture failed completely.

Next the Son, the Stunning-Cantab:
He suggested curves of beauty,
Curves pervading all his figure,
Which the eye might follow onward,
Till they centred in the breast-pin,
Centred in the golden breast-pin.
He had learnt it all from Ruskin
(Author of "The Stones of Venice",
"Seven Lamps of Architecture",
"Modern Painters", and some others);
And perhaps he had not fully

115

Understood his author's meaning;
But, whatever was the reason,
All was fruitless, as the picture
Ended in an utter failure.

Next to him the eldest daughter:
She suggested very little,
Only asked if he would take her
With her look of "passive beauty".

Her idea of passive beauty
Was a squinting of the left-eye,
Was a drooping of the right-eye,
Was a smile that went up sideways
To the corner of the nostrils.

Hiawatha, when she asked him,
Took no notice of the question,
Looked as if he hadn't heard it;
But, when pointedly appealed to,
Smiled in his peculiar manner,
Coughed and said it "didn't matter",
Bit his lip and changed the subject.

Nor in this was he mistaken,
As the picture failed completely.

So in turn the other sisters.

Last, the youngest son was taken:
Very rough and thick his hair was,
Very round and red his face was,
Very dusty was his jacket,
Very fidgety his manner.
And his overbearing sisters
Called him names he disapproved of:
Called him Johnny, "Daddy's Darling",
Called him Jacky, "Scrubby School-boy",
And, so awful was the picture,
In comparison the others
Seemed, to one's bewildered fancy,
To have partially succeeded.

Finally my Hiawatha
Tumbled all the tribe together,
("Grouped" is not the right expression),
And, as happy chance would have it
Did at last obtain a picture
Where the faces all succeeded:
Each came out a perfect likeness.

Then they joined and all abused it,
Unrestrainedly abused it,
As the worst and ugliest picture
They could possibly have dreamed of.

116

"Giving one such strange expressions—
Sullen, stupid, pert expressions.
Really anyone would take us
(Anyone that did not know us)
For the most unpleasant people!"
(Hiawatha seemed to think so,
Seemed to think it not unlikely.)
All together rang their voices,
Angry, loud, discordant voices,
As of dogs that howl in concert,
As of cats that wail in chorus.

But my Hiawatha's patience,
His politeness and his patience,
Unaccountably had vanished,
And he left that happy party.
Neither did he leave them slowly,
With the calm deliberation,
The intense deliberation
Of a photographic artist:
But he left them in a hurry,
Left them in a mighty hurry,
Stating that he would not stand it,
Stating in emphatic language
What he'd be before he'd stand it.
Hurriedly he packed his boxes:
Hurriedly the porter trundled
On a barrow all his boxes:
Hurriedly he took his ticket:
Hurriedly the train received him:
Thus departed Hiawatha.

117

III

The Ladye's History
Part of The Legend of "Scotland"

"The Legend of 'Scotland'" was published posthumously in *The Lewis Carroll Picture Book* (1899) by Stuart Dodgson Collingwood. Lewis Carroll pretends that the legend was written down in 1325, though the language is simplified so that the daughters of the Bishop of Durham, for whose amusement it was written, would be able to understand it.

"On a dewie autum evening, mighte have been seen, pacing yn the grounds harde by Aucklande Castell, a yong Ladye of a stiff and perky manner, yet not ill to look on, nay, one mighte saye, faire to a degree, save that haply that hadde been untrue.

"That yong Ladye, O miserable Man, was I" (whereon I demanded on what score shee held mee miserable, and shee replied, yt mattered not). "I plumed myself yn those tymes on my exceeding not soe much beauty as loftinesse of Figure, and gretely desired that some Painter might paint my picture: but they ever were too high, not yn skyll I trow, byt yn charges." (At thys I most humbly enquired at what charge the then Painters wrought, but shee loftily affirmed that money-matters were vulgar and that shee knew not, no, nor cared.)

"Now yt chaunced that a certyn Artist, hight Lorenzo, came toe that Quarter, having wyth hym a merveillous machine called by men a Chimera (that ys, a fabulous and wholly incredible thing;) where wyth hee took manie pictures, each yn a single stroke of Tyme, whiles that a Man might name 'John, the son of Robin' (I asked her, what might a stroke of Tyme bee, but shee, frowning, answered not.)

"He yt was that undertook my Picture: yn which I mainly required one thyng, that yt should bee at full-length, for yn none other way mighte my Loftiness bee trulie set forth. Nevertheless, though hee took manie Pictures, yet all fayled yn thys: for some, beginning at the Hedde, reeched not toe the Feet;

118

others, taking yn the Feet, yet left out the Hedde; whereof the former were a grief unto myself, and the latter a Laughing-Stocke unto others.

"At these thyngs I justly fumed, having at the first been frendly unto hym (though yn sooth hee was dull),.and oft smote him gretely on the Eares, rending from hys Hedde certyn Locks, whereat crying out hee was wont toe saye that I made hys lyfe a burden untoe hym, whych thyng I not so much doubted as highlie rejoyced yn.

"At the last hee counselled thys, that a Picture shoulde bee made, showing so much skyrt as mighte reesonably bee gotte yn, and a Notice set below toe thys effect: 'Item, two yards and a Half Ditto, and then the Feet.' But thys no Whit contented mee, and thereon I shut hym ynto the Cellar, where hee remaned three Weeks, growing dayly thinner and thinner, till at the last hee floted up and downe like a Feather.

"Now yt fell at thys tyme, as I questioned hym on a certyn Day, yf hee woulde nowe take mee at full-length, and hee replying untoe mee, yn a little moning Voyce, lyke a Gnat, one chaunced to open the Door: whereat the Draft bore hym uppe ynto a Cracke of the Cieling, and I remained awaytyng hym, holding uppe my Torche, until such tyme as I also faded ynto a Ghost, yet stickyng untoe the Wall."

Then did my Loorde and the Companie haste down ynto the Cellar, for to see thys straunge sight, to whych place when they came, my Loorde bravely drew hys sword, loudly crying "Death!" (though to whom or what he explained not); then some went yn, but the more part hung back, urging on those yn front, not soe largely bye example, as Words of cheer: yet at last all entered, my Loorde last.

Then they removed from the wall the Casks and other stuff, and founde the sayd Ghost, dredful toe relate, yet extant on the Wall, at which horrid sight such screems were raysed as yn these days are seldom or never herde: some faynted, others bye large drafts of Beer saved themselves from that Extremity, yet were they scarcely alive for Feer.

Then dyd the Ladye speak unto them yn suchwise:—

> "Here I bee, and here I byde,
> Till such tyme as yt betyde
> That a Ladye of thys place,
> Lyke to mee yn name and face,
> (Though my name bee never known,
> My initials shall bee shown),
> Shall be fotograffed [1] aright—

---

[1] "Fotograffed" is extraordinarily "modern" spelling for what is meant to be early fourteenth-century English. (H.G.)

119

Hedde and Feet bee both yn sight—
Then my face shall disappeer,
Nor agayn affrite you heer."

Then sayd Matthew Dixon unto her, "Wherefore holdest thou uppe that Torche?" to whych shee answered, "Candles Gyve Light": but none understood her.

After thys a thyn Voyce sang from overhedde:—

"Yn the Auckland Castell cellar,
Long, long ago,
I was shut—a brisk yong feller—
Woe, woe, ah woe!
To take her at full-lengthe
I never hadde the strengthe
Tempore (and soe I tell her,)
Praeterito!

(Yn thys Chorus they durst none joyn, seeing that Latyn was untoe them a Tongue unknown).

"She was hard—oh, she was cruel—
Long, long ago,
Starved mee here—not even gruel—
No, believe mee, no!—
Frae Scotland could I flee,
I'd gie my last bawbee,—
Arrah, bhoys, fair play's a jhewel,
Lave, me, darlints, goe!"

Then my Loorde, putting bye hys Sworde, (whych was layd up thereafter, yn memory of soe grete Bravery,) bade hys Butler fetch hym presentlie a Vessel of Beer, whych when yt was broughte at hys nod, (nor, as hee merrily sayd, hys "nod, and Bec, and wreathed smyle,") hee drank hugelie thereof: "for why?" quoth hee, "surely a Bec ys no longer a Bec, when yt ys Dry."

IV

A Photographer's Day Out

"A Photographer's Day Out" was published in *The South Shields Amateur Magazine*, 1860.

I AM shaken, and sore, and stiff, and bruised. As I have told you many times already, I haven't the least idea how it happened and there is no use in plaguing me with any more questions about it. Of course, if you wish it, I can read you an extract from my diary, giving a full account of the events of yesterday, but if you expect to find any clue to the mystery in *that*, I fear you are doomed to be disappointed.

AUGUST 23, *Tuesday.* They say that we Photographers are a blind race at best; that we learn to look at even the prettiest faces as so much light and shade; that we seldom admire, and never love. This is a delusion I long to break through—if I could only find a young lady to photograph, realizing *my* ideal of beauty—above all, if her name should be—(why is it, I wonder, that I dote on the name Amelia more than any other word in the English language?) —I feel sure that I could shake off this cold, philosophic lethargy.

The time has come at last. Only this evening I fell in with young Harry Glover in the Haymarket—"Tubbs!" he shouted, slapping me familiarly on the back, "my Uncle wants you down tomorrow at his Villa, camera and all!"

"But I don't know your Uncle", I replied, with my characteristic caution. (N.B. If I have a virtue, it is quiet, gentlemanly caution.)

"Never mind, old boy, he knows all about *you.* You be off by the early train, and take your whole kit of bottles, for you'll find lots of faces to uglify, and—"

"Ca'n't go", I said rather gruffly, for the extent of the job alarmed me, and I wished to cut him short, having a decided objection to talking slang in the public streets.

"Well, they'll be precious cut up about it, that's all", said Harry, with rather a blank face, "and my cousin Amelia—"

"Don't say another word!" I cried enthusiastically, "I'll go!" And as my

121

omnibus came by at the moment, I jumped in and rattled off before he had recovered his astonishment at my change of manner. So it is settled, and to-morrow I am to see an Amelia, and—Oh Destiny, what hast thou in store for me?

AUGUST 24, *Wednesday.* A glorious morning. Packed in a great hurry, luckily breaking only two bottles and three glasses in doing so. Arrived at Rosemary Villa as the party were sitting down to breakfast. Father, mother, two sons from school, a host of children from the nursery and the inevitable B A B Y.

But how shall I describe the daughter? Words are powerless; nothing but a Talbotype could do it. Her nose was in beautiful perspective—her mouth wanting perhaps the least possible fore-shortening—but the exquisite half-tints on the cheek would have blinded one to any defects, and as to the high light on her chin, it was (photographically speaking) perfection. Oh! what a picture she would have made if fate had not—but I am anticipating.

There was a Captain Flanaghan present—

I am aware that the preceding paragraph is slightly abrupt, but when I reached that point, I remembered that the idiot actually believed himself engaged to Amelia (*my* Amelia!) I choked, and could get no further. His figure, I am willing to admit, was good: some might have admired his face; but what is face or figure without brains?

My own figure is perhaps a *little* inclined to the robust; in stature I am none of your military giraffes—but why should I describe myself? My photograph (done by myself) will be sufficient evidence to the world.

The breakfast, no doubt, was good, but I knew not what I ate or drank; I lived for Amelia only, and as I gazed on that peerless brow, those chiseled features, I clenched my fist in an involuntary transport (upsetting my coffee-cup in doing so), and mentally exclaimed, "I will photograph that woman, or perish in the attempt!"

After breakfast the work of the day commenced, which I will here briefly record.

Picture 1.—Paterfamilias. This I wanted to try again, but they all declared it would do very well, and had "just his usual expression"; though unless his usual expression was that of a man with a bone in his throat, endeavouring to alleviate the agony of choking by watching the end of his nose with both eyes, I must admit that this was too favourable a statement of the case.

Picture 2.—Materfamilias. She told us with a simper, as she sat down, that she "had been very fond of theatricals in her youth", and that she "wished to be taken in a favourite Shakespearean character." What the character was, after long and anxious thought on the subject, I have given up as a hopeless mystery, not knowing any one of his heroines in whom an attitude of such

122

spasmodic energy could have been combined with a face of such blank indifference, or who could have been thought appropriately costumed in a blue silk gown, with a Highland scarf over one shoulder, a ruffle of Queen Elizabeth's time round the throat, and a hunting-whip.

Picture 3.—17th sitting. Placed the baby in profile. After waiting till the usual kicking had subsided, uncovered the lens. The little wretch instantly threw its head back, luckily only an inch, as it was stopped by the nurse's nose, establishing the infant's claim to "first blood" (to use a sporting phrase). This, of course, gave *two* eyes to the result, something that might be called a nose, and an unnaturally wide mouth. Called it a full-face accordingly and went on to

Picture 4.—The three younger girls, as they would have appeared, if by any possibility a black dose could have been administered to each of them at the same moment, and the three tied together by the hair before the expression produced by the medicine had subsided from any of their faces. Of course, I kept this view of the subject to myself, and merely said that "it reminded me of a picture of the three Graces", but the sentence ended in an involuntary groan, which I had the greatest difficulty in converting into a cough.

Picture 5.—This was to have been the great artistic triumph of the day; a family group, designed by the two parents, and combining the domestic with the allegorical. It was intended to represent the baby being crowned with flowers, by the united efforts of the children, regulated by the advice of the father, under the personal superintendence of the mother; and to combine with this the secondary meaning of "Victory transferring her laurel crown to Innocence, with Resolution, Independence, Faith, Hope and Charity, assisting in the graceful task, while Wisdom looks benignly on, and smiles approval!" Such, I say, was the *intention*; the result, to any unprejudiced observer, was capable of but one interpretation—that the baby was in a fit—that the mother (doubtless under some erroneous notions of the principles of Human Anatomy), was endeavouring to recover it by bringing the crown of its head in contact with its chest—that the two boys, seeing no prospect for the infant but immediate destruction, were tearing out some locks of its hair as mementos of the fatal event—that two of the girls were waiting for a chance at the baby's hair, and employing the time in strangling the third—and that the father, in despair at the extraordinary conduct of his family, had stabbed himself, and was feeling for his pencil-case, to make a memorandum of having done so.

All this time I had no opportunity of asking my Amelia for a sitting, but during luncheon I succeeded in finding one, and, after introducing the subject of photographs in general, I turned to her and said, "before the day is

123

out, Miss Amelia, I hope to do myself the honour of coming to *you* for a negative."

With a sweet smile she replied "Certainly, Mr. Tubbs. There is a cottage near here, that I wish you would try after luncheon, and when you've done that, I shall be at your service."

"Faix! an' I hope she'll give you a decoisive one!" broke in that awkward Captain Flanaghan, "wo'n't you, Mely Darlint?" "I trust so, Captain Flanaghan", I interposed with great dignity; but all politeness is wasted on that animal; he broke into great "haw! haw!" and Amelia and I could hardly refrain from laughing at his folly. She, however, with ready tact turned it off, saying to the bear "come, come, Captain, we mustn't be *too* hard on him!" (Hard on *me*! on *me*! bless thee, Amelia.)

The sudden happiness of that moment nearly overcame me; tears rose to my eyes as I thought, "the wish of a Life is accomplished! I shall photograph an Amelia!" Indeed, I almost think I should have gone down on my knees to thank her, had not the table-cloth interfered with my so doing, and had I not known what a difficult position it is to recover from.

However, I seized an opportunity towards the close of the meal to give utterance to my overwrought feelings: turning towards Amelia, who was sitting next to me, I had just murmured the words "there beats in this bosom a heart", when a general silence warned me to leave the sentence unfinished. With the most admirable presence of mind she said "Some tart, did you say, Mr. Tubbs? Captain Flanaghan, may I trouble you to cut Mr. Tubbs some of that tart?"

"It's nigh done," said the Captain, poking his great head almost into it; "will I send him the dish, Mely?"

"No, Sir!" I interrupted, with a look that ought to have crushed him, but he only grinned and said, "Don't be modest now, Tubbs, me bhoy, sure there's plenty more in the larder."

Amelia was looking anxiously at me, so I swallowed my rage—and the tart.

Luncheon over, after receiving directions by which to find the cottage, I attached to my camera the hood used for developing pictures in the open air, placed it over my shoulder, and set out for the hill which had been pointed out to me.

My Amelia was sitting in the window working, as I passed with the machine; the Irish idiot was with her. In reply to my look of undying affection, she said anxiously, "I'm sure that's too heavy for you, Mr. Tubbs. Wo'n't you have a boy to carry it?"

"Or a donkey?" giggled the captain.

I pulled up short, and faced round, feeling that now, if ever, the dignity of

Man, and the liberty of the subject, must be asserted. To *her* I merely said, "thanks, thanks!" kissing my hand as I spoke; then, fixing my eyes on the idiot at her side, I hissed through my clenched teeth, *"we shall meet again, Captain!"*

"Sure, I hope so, Tubbs", said the unconscious blockhead, "sharp six is the dinner hour, mind!" A cold shiver passed over me; I had made my great effort, and had *failed*; I shouldered my camera again, and strode moodily on.

Two steps, and I was myself again; *her* eyes, I knew, were upon me, and once more I trod the gravel with an elastic tread. What mattered to me, in that moment, the whole tribe of captains? should *they* disturb my equanimity?

The hill was nearly a mile from the house, and I reached it tired and breathless. Thoughts of Amelia, however, bore me up. I selected the best point of view for the cottage, so as to include a farmer and cow in the picture, cast one fond look toward the distant villa, and, muttering, "Amelia, 'tis for thee!" removed the lid of the lens; in 1 minute and 40 seconds I replaced it: "it is over!" I cried in uncontrollable excitement, "Amelia, thou art mine!"

Eagerly, tremblingly, I covered my head with the hood, and commenced the development. Trees rather misty—well! the wind had blown them about a little; *that* wouldn't show much—the farmer? well, *he* had walked on a yard or two, and I should be sorry to state how many arms and legs he appeared with—never mind! call him a spider, a centipede, anything—the cow? I must, however reluctantly, confess that the cow had three heads, and though such an animal may be curious, it is *not* picturesque. However, there could be no mistake about the cottage; its chimneys were all that could be desired, and, "all things considered", I thought, "Amelia will—"

At this point my soliloquy was interrupted by a tap on the shoulder, more peremptory than suggestive. I withdrew myself from the hood, need I say with what quiet dignity? and turned upon the stranger. He was a thick-built man, vulgar in dress, repulsive in expression, and carried a straw in his mouth: his companion outdid him in these peculiarities. "Young man", began the first, "ye're trespassing here, and ya mun take yourself off, and no bones about it." I need hardly say that I took no notice of this remark, but took up the bottle of hypo-sulphite of soda, and proceeded to fix the picture; he tried to stop me; I resisted: the negative fell, and was broken. I remember nothing further, except that I have an indistinct notion that I hit somebody.

If you can find anything in what I have just read to you to account for my present condition, you are welcome to do so; but, as I before remarked, all I can tell you is that I am shaken, and sore, and stiff, and bruised, and that how I came so I haven't the faintest idea.

DATE DUE

GAYLORD			PRINTED IN U.S.A.